# Collectanea Hermetica Volume II

# THE
# DIVINE
## *PYMANDER*

OF

*Hermes Mercurius Trismegistus,*

In XVII. Books.

Translated formerly out of the *Arabick* into *Greek*, and thence into *Latine*, and *Dutch*, and now out of the Original into *English*;

By that Learned Divine Doctor *Everard*.

---

*London*, Printed by *Robert White*, for *Tho. Brewster*, and *Greg. Moule*, at the Three Bibles in the *Poultrey*, under *Mildreds* Church, 1650.

Title page for *The Divine Pymander* (1650).

# COLLECTANEA HERMETICA

### EDITED BY

## W. WYNN WESTCOTT, M.B., D.P.H.

*(Supreme Magus of the Rosicrucian Society.*
*Master of the Quatuor Coronati Lodge.)*

### VOLUME II.

—

# THE DIVINE
# PYMANDER

OF

# HERMES

## 1650

WITH A PREFACE BY THE EDITOR

**2011**
**GOLDEN DAWN RESEARCH TRUST**

# Collectanea Hermetica
## Vol. II: Divine Pymander of Hermes

●○○○○○○●●●

ISBN: 978-1-9269820-1-4.

First published as Volume II of the *Collectanea Hermetica*
by Theosophical Publishing Society, 1894.

Revised and Corrected Edition.
First Printing, 2012.

**GOLDEN DAWN RESEARCH TRUST**
P.O. Box 15964 Austin, Texas 78761-5964 USA

# Contents

# ILLUSTRATIONS

# A NOTE

# "COLLECTANEA HERMETICA."

---

IN 1875 the creation of the Theosophical Society offered a way of escape for those seekers after Truth who could accept neither a dogmatic brand of Christianity nor a dull and barren Rationalism, and for whom Spiritualism was intellectually inadequate. For a decade Madame Blavatsky's emphasis on Eastern religion and thought was enough, but a growing number of English members sought to study—in both theory and practice—the Hermetic Tradition of the West. Their demands were finally met in 1887 by the founding of the Hermetic Order of the Golden Dawn, a secret Order based upon the precepts and practices of the Rosicrucians of the seventeenth century, and whose members were required to follow a disciplined course of study. With a high proportion of articulate and cultured men and women among its members it was inevitable that the Golden Dawn should produce lasting memorials, and while the splendid rituals created by S.L.M. Mathers are the best known of these, the true value of the Order appeared in the series of manuals edited by the Order's founder, William Wynn Westcott.

The ten volumes of Westcott's *Collectanea Hermetica* appeared over the three years from 1893 to 1896 when the Golden Dawn was at its peak. It was a remarkable series providing guides for the public and, virtually, textbooks for members on almost all the major pursuits of the Order: on Alchemy, the Kabbalah, Gnosticism, the Mystery Religions and Egyptian traditions. In every volume the intellectual integrity of the authors is evident, as is an eagerness to bring academic respectability to subjects derided by their contemporaries. Westcott and his colleagues were pioneers in the study of "rejected knowledge", and the gradual acceptance today of the real value of research in such fields is a vindication of their efforts and justification enough for the long overdue rescue of their work from an ill-deserved neglect.

ROBERT A. GILBERT,
*Bristol,* 1983.

# FOREWORD

# "DIVINE PYMANDER."

———

29. THEN said Pimander, "This is the Mystery that to this day is hidden, and kept secret; for Nature being mingled with Man brought forth a Wonder most wonderful; for he having the Nature of the Harmony of the Seven, from him whom I told thee, the Fire and the Spirit, Nature continued not, but forth with brought forth seven Men all Males and Females and sublime, or on high, according to the Natures of the Seven Governors." (From the Second Book, called *Poemander*.)

*The Divine Pymander of Hermes Mercurius Trismegistus in XVII Books* was published in 1650 by John Everard. Translated from Marsilio Ficino's Latin translation of 1471, Everard's work represents the first English translation of the *Corpus Hermeticum* (the "Hermetic body of writings"), the foundational documents of the Hermetic tradition, said to have been written by Hermes the Thrice-Great, an avatar or living embodiment of the god Hermes-Thoth. Hermes Trismegistus was said to be an ancient Egyptian priest and magician who was credited with writing forty-two books on esoteric wisdom collectively known as the Hermetic literature or *Hermetica*. The *Pymander* (Ποιμάνδρης), also spelled *Poemandres*, *Poemander* or *Pimander* is one of the chapters in the *Corpus Hermeticum*. It means "Man-

Shepherd," alluding to God as Divine Mind, and in another sense as "the Good Shepherd" or "Shepherd of Men."

While the Hermetic books were not markedly different from other contemporary texts on magical philosophy, these works became extremely important because of the high position given to them by Renaissance thinkers and magicians. They were also judged to be acceptable to the Christian church for nearly 1,500 years—highly unusual for books written by an Egyptian Initiate who was named after a pagan god. And because of this remarkable acceptance, the books have played an important role in Western culture ever since.

The various Greek texts which became known as the *Corpus Hermeticum* were collected into a single book during the Byzantine era. In 1460 a monk brought a copy to Cosimo de' Medici, an avid philosopher and one of the most powerful and influential nobles in northern Italy. Three years later, de Medici commissioned Marsilio Ficino, a philosopher, scholar, and magician, to translate the book. The works of Hermes Trismegistus were considered so important that Ficino had to put aside translation of the entire works of Plato until after the *Corpus Hermeticum* had been translated in 1463. It was reprinted numerous times over the next century and a half.

The reason why the church did not attempt to eradicate the Hermetic literature, as it had done with other pagan books, was because many of the spiritual ideas embraced by the books were very similar to Christian principles. Thinking that the Hermetic books were much older than they actually were, church officials thought that they were the work of an enlightened ancient pagan who envisioned the forthcoming Christian "truths." Had they known that the books were penned by a not-so-ancient Hellenistic pagan thinker, they would have no doubt branded the texts as heresy and committed them to the fire.

It is now known that the *Hermetica* was not written by

a single individual, but rather by different authors living in Egypt sometime before the end of the third century c.e. This material had its roots in Platonism and the religious traditions of the Hellenistic Middle East—it was produced by the same religious, philosophical fervor that produced Neoplatonism, Gnosticism, and Christianity and the writings associated with these diverse traditions. The Hermetic texts display a composite origin that blended Egyptian piety with Hellenic philosophy and Jewish influences.

Adding to the complexity of the material, the teachings contained within these books show two different philosophical viewpoints—one that tends toward the pessimism of Gnostic Dualism, and the other, more prevalent perspective that displays a holistic optimism. The inclination toward Dualism can be found in passages such as the following:

> 44. Nothing good upon Earth; nothing evil in Heaven.
> 45. God is good, man is evil.
> 65. The Generation of Man is Corruption. ...
> 74. The Earth is brutish, the Heaven is reasonable or rational.
> 80. What is God? The immutable or unalterable Good.
> 81. What is Man? An unchangeable Evil.
>
> (From The First Book, called *Hermes Trismegistus*.)

Contrast this with the optimistic approach evident in the bulk of the literature, much more typical of the Hermetic approach, wherein the human body and all of Nature was seen as wondrous examples of God's creative majesty and ingenuity:

> 21. I would it were possible for thee, O my Son, to have wings, and to fly into the Air, and being taken up in the midst, between Heaven and Earth, to see the stability of the Earth, the fluidness of the Sea, the courses of the Rivers, the largeness of the Air, the sharpness or swiftness

of the Fire, the motion of the Stars; and the speediness of the Heaven, by which it goeth round about all these.

22. O Son, what a happy sight it were, at one instant, to see all these, that which is unmovable moved, and that which is hidden appear and be manifest.

23. And if thou wilt see and behold this Workman, even by mortal things that are upon Earth, and in the deep, consider, O Son, how Man is made and framed in the Womb; and examine diligently the skill and cunning of the Workman, and learn who it was that wrought and fashioned the beautiful and Divine shape of Man. ...

(From The Fifth Book, called *That God is Not Manifest And Yet Most Manifest.*)

The books of *Corpus Hermeticum* were part of a Second century Pagan cultural revival that was diverse, syncretic, and academic. This movement embraced the works of the Neoplatonists, the Orphics, the Gnostics and the Pythagoreans, and resulted in the creation of similar visionary writings such as *The Chaldean Oracles*. The Jewish influence upon these texts is undeniable, as demonstrated by a vocabulary that bears striking similarities with the Greek Bible and the use of such phrases as "Lord and Father" (The Fifth Book, line 9). A cosmology inspired by the Book of Genesis is evident in both The Second Book (*Poemander*) and The Third Book (*The Holy Sermon*). The Egyptian flavor is here as well: the Hermetic God is called "the All and the One," and he is described as "his own father" and "his own mother" appellations which are common throughout the invocations of the Pyramid Texts and other Khemetic writings.

Ancient Hermetics viewed the concept of God or the gods in diverse, often eclectic ways, prompting author George Stock to describe Hermetic religion as "polytheistic, pantheistic, and monotheistic" (*Encyclopædia of Religion and Ethics*, Vol. VI, 629). Nevertheless the idea of a highest

"God" recurs throughout the Hermetic literature, and is often represented as Intellect or Nous, existing within the highest heaven or ideal level of reality, not unlike the Judeo-Christian concept of God. This God is both immanent (within everything) and transcendent (beyond everything) and is the Creator of the manifest Universe as we know it.

The texts of *The Divine Pymander* are written in a format that marks them as foundational teaching "gospels" for Hermetic communities. They are presented in the form of a dialogue, a favorite structure of didactic writing in the ancient world, wherein a teacher enlightens a questioning student. The texts take the form of divine revelation or apocalyptic vision received by the founder of the tradition. But as author G.R.S. Mead tells us in his "Commentary on Pymander" from *Thrice Greatest Hermes*, Vol. II:

> That founder, however, is not so much a historical personage as the personification of a teaching-power or grade of spiritual illumination—in other words, of one who had reached the Hermetic or rather "Thrice-greatest" state of consciousness or enlightenment.
>
> This stage of enlightenment is characterized by a heightening of the spiritual intuition that made the mystic capable of receiving the first touch of cosmic consciousness, and of retaining it in his physical memory when he returned to the normal state. The setting forth of the divine teaching is thus naturally in the form of apocalyptic scenes but of an ordered and logical nature. The treatise purports to be a setting forth of the spiritual "Epopteia" ("seeing beyond") of the Inner Mysteries, the Vision revealed by the Great Initiator or Master Hierophant, the One Mind of all-masterhood.
>
> This Vision, as we are told by many seers and prophets of the time, was incapable of being set forth by "tongue of flesh" in its own proper terms, since it transcended the consciousness of normal humanity. Being in itself a

living potent, intelligible reality, apart from all forms either material or intellectual in any way known to man, it pervaded his very being and made his whole nature respond to a new key of truth, or rather, vibrate in a higher octave so to say, where all things while remaining the same, received a new interpretation and intensity.

Mead, a skilled translator with a firm understanding of the meaning of these often ambiguous texts, published his own translation of the *Corpus Hermeticum* in the Second Volume of his *Thrice Greatest Hermes* (London, 1906). Mead recognized the power in these archaic writings, as did Everard, Ficino, and de' Medici before him. Mead's version, now in the public domain, is undoubtedly a more accurate translation than Everard's, but today neither version is considered a reliable rendition of the original textual material—for that readers can refer to Brian Copenhaver's *Hermetica* (1995). But the mythic power and grace of these ancient revelations are not lost in either the post-Reformation language of Everard or the post-Victorian language of Mead. This why William Wynn Wescott included the Everard version in his *Collectanea Hermetica* series, published in 1894.

Westcott was the Supreme Magus of the Societas Rosicruciana in Anglia (a Rosicrucian fraternity of learning and research for Master Masons), the Worshipful Master of the Quattuor Coronati Lodge (the foremost British Masonic Lodge of Research), and the primary creator of the Hermetic Order of the Golden Dawn in 1888. Publication of *Collectanea Hermetica* was sponsored by the Theosophical Society with Westcott as editor in his public role as Supreme Magus of the SRIA. But as author Adam Forrest has pointed out, getting this foundational Hermetic material into the hands of eager students:

Was in fact a part of Westcott's Work in his duties as

a Chief of the Golden Dawn and its Inner Order Rosæ Rubeæ et Aureæ Crucis (the Order of the Rose of Ruby and the Cross of Gold). He contributed introductions and commentaries to various of the volumes in the Collection under his Order Mottos as "Sapere Aude, Fra. R.R. et A.C.," "S.A.," "Non Omnis Moriar," and "N.O.M.; R.R. et A.C.," and his associates in preparing the series were his fellow Golden Dawn Adepts, Florence Farr and Percy Bullock, who contributed translations and notes not under their mundane names but under their Mottos—Farr (V.H. Sor. Sapientia Sapienti Dona Data) as "S.S.D.D.," and "S.S.D.D.–R.R. et A.C.", and Bullock (V.H. Fra. Levavi Oculos) as "L.O."

Over the course of four decades Westcott published a seemingly inexhaustible stream of articles for Masonic journals, books, papers, translations and commentaries on Hermeticism, Alchemy and Kabbalah. Much of his work directly benefited his students and fellow Initiates within the Golden Dawn. It should come as no surprise then, that certain words and phrases from Everard's *The Divine Pymander of Hermes Mercurius Trismegistus in XVII Books* sound very similar, if not identical in some instances, to language used by Westcott and his companions. Echoes of *The Divine Pymander* reverberate throughout the initiation ceremonies of the Golden Dawn. For example in the 0°=0° Grade the Hiereus tells the Neophyte that:

> The Seed of Wisdom is Sown in Silence and Grows in Darkness and Mystery.

In the Seventh Book, called *His Secret Sermon in the Mount of Regeneration, and the Profession of Silence*, Hermes Trismegistus tells his son Tat:

> O Son, this Wisdom is to be understood in silence, and

the Seed is the true Good. [...] Wherefore this is not taught, but hid in silence.

In another example, the "Adoration to the Lord of the Universe" from the Neophyte Ceremony shows a sentence taken verbatim from *The Divine Pymander*:

> Holy art Thou, Lord of the Universe.
> Holy art Thou, whom Nature hath not formed.
> Holy art Thou, The Vast and Mighty One.
> Lord of the Light and of the Darkness.

Compare this to a passage from the Second Book (*Poemander*):

> 86. Holy is God, the Father of All Things.
> 87. Holy is God, Whose Will is Performed and Accomplished by His Own Powers.
> 88. Holy is God, that Determineth to be Known, and is Known of His Own, or Those that are His.
> 89. Holy art Thou, that by Thy Word hast established all Things.
> 90. Holy art Thou, of Whom all Nature is the Image.
> 91. Holy art Thou, Whom Nature hath not Formed.
> 92. Holy art Thou, that art Stronger than all Power.
> 93. Holy art Thou, that art Greater than all Excellency.
> 94. Holy art Thou, Who art Better than all Praise.

The books contained in *The Divine Pymander* are expressions of profound spiritual experiences—divine revelations and prophetic visionary realities that inspired their authors, motivating them to communicate such experiences to others. They are conveyances of Hermetic Gnosis which can only be comprehended by those who are open to such initiatory experiences. These texts describe the Hermetic paradigm of reality—cosmic principles; the nature and creation of the universe, the nature and composition of the human soul; the nature of other spiritual beings; the dual nature of reality (physical versus spiritual); the rule of Fate over the lives of humanity and how Fate may be overcome; man's desire to know God, and the way to achieve spiritual rebirth (called "regeneration" by the *Hermetica* and "born again" in modern religious terminology). This is evident in the Second Book of *Poemander* which begins with a dream-like vision, where an entity who calls himself Poemander introduces himself to the anonymous narrator of the story and begins to relate the story of Creation.

The Hermetic texts, seen as proof of an ancient wisdom tradition that predated Christianity, shook the philosophical systems of the late medieval world. As a result of this fortuitous mistake in dating the texts, combined with a fresh and positive interpretation of "Natural Magic" by Ficino, the subject of magic, once banished into the subterranean darkness by the church, ascended to the new light of day as a learned topic for scholarly, philosophical discussion. But it was not to last. The drastic overhaul of Christianity that occurred during the Reformation and Counter-Reformation resulted in the erection of new barricades between the supposedly "separate" realms of magic and religion.

It would take the Occult Revival of the 19th century, and magicians such as William Wynn Westcott, to poke holes in these capricious barriers and make the language and concepts of the *Hermetica* accessible, and in fact central, to the post-medieval magic of the Western Esoteric Tradition.

Chic and Sandra Tabatha Cicero,
*Elfers, FL,* 2011.

# PREFACE

## TO THE

# "DIVINE PYMANDER."

---

This volume contains the English translation by Dr. Everard, 1650, of seventeen tracts (of which the *Pymander* is one) attributed to Hermes Trismegistos, otherwise Mercurius Termaximus, or in the Egyptian language, Thoth, or Taautes or Tat. Of this Hermes no reliable historical details have come down to us, but many of the ancient authors have referred to Hermes as an inspired teacher who instructed the priests and rulers of the Egyptian nation at a time almost certainly anterior to that commonly associated with Moses. It has been asserted by men who have been called learned, that this Hermes was really identical with Enoch, and by others he has been identified as Gautama—the Buddha. If the name HERMES be taken and the suffix "ES" be neglected, and the word formed of the letters H, R, M, be traced through Chaldee, Coptic, Greek and Latin forms, an analogy will be observed between Hermes, and Hiram the hero of the myth of Freemasonry, a symbolical system of morals and theosophy which is but a reconstruction of a portion of the Ancient Mysteries. Now the Mysteries of Egypt, named Osirian, Serapian and Isiac, are the most ancient known to us, and were the parents of the Eleusinian Mysteries of the Greeks. All these Mysteries were initiations, or forms of Esoteric instruction relating to theosophy, properly so-called, that is the knowledge of divine powers and beings, and the connection between Man and the

Divine Source from which he is animated and inspired. Now the tracts which have come down to us, associated with the name of Hermes as their author, are all concerned with that arcane wisdom which was developed in three directions:—Theosophy,—religious and ethical teaching; Alchymy—the relation of the material to the spiritual and the transmutations of the former into the latter; and Magic—the employment of the higher powers latent in man upon the physical plane. In the Hermetic tracts these several objects are not kept distinct, but on the contrary, are almost invariably combined; hence the great value to a true student of Occultism of these very ancient writings. It is not of course asserted that the *Pymander* or other Hermetic work has come down to us in its original form, but it is contended that although varied in many a line and possibly in many a doctrine by the Neo-Platonists and Alexandrian school, and perhaps in later days by Christian philosophers, the *Pymander*, *Aureus*, *etc.*, do yet enshrine the very old Egyptian ideals, and are almost the only remains now existing of the Wisdom of the hierophants of the Nile valley.

Kenealy has asserted that the name Hermes meant in the ancient Egyptian language—an interpreter, and in a certain sense the later Hermes of the Greeks and the Mercurius of the Romans conveyed the same notion; this author, in his quaint conceit of Twelve Saviours, places Hermes under the name of Thoth as the Sixth Messiah, and assigns to him the era of 1800 years before Christ.

This Thoth, as an Egyptian divinity, is often represented as a human form with an Ibis head; now the bird Ibis was notable as being the great destroyer of snakes, and the snake as apart from the regal serpent, was an emblem of evil, sin and error; hence the Snake Destroyer fits in well with the character of Hermes as a Teacher of divine truths, which would serve to crush and beat down evil thoughts and actions.

The earliest record of the title Trismegistos, as applied to this Egyptian sage, is found in Greek authors who lived some four centuries B.C. The Neo-Platonists, who were of Greek culture, looked upon Hermes as the embodied LOGOS, or Word or Manifestation of the Divine Spirit. The title may have had reference to his mastery over the Three Divine sciences—Theosophy, Alchymy and Magic—as indeed is stated in paragraph twelve of the Emerald Tablet assigned to him, of which the words following are an old Latin version:

*Itaque vocatus sum Hermes Trismegistus, habens tres partes divinæ philosophiæ totius mundi*, that is—"possessing the three parts of the divine philosophy of the whole world."

The name Pymander is of Greek and not Egyptian type; it is variously spelled Pimander and Poemandres. Its derivation appears to be from *poimēn*—a shepherd, and *anēr*, genitive plural *andrōn*, and so the Guide of Man, Shepherd of men, and is nearly equivalent to Messiah. In this tract the Pymander is giving instruction to Hermes the sage, in the capacity of Divine teacher to human pupil. A parallel conception is seen in the Bhagavad Gita, where Krishna teaches Arjuna.

Blavatsky in *The Secret Doctrine* refers to the *Pymander* as the "Thought Divine," the Inspired Teacher of that Race—Vol. I, 63; and again at page 74, she speaks of Pymander as "the oldest and most spiritual of the Logoi of the Western continent." She also notices the possibility of a Hebrew derivation from PI, meaning a mouth, and command, or instruction. I observe that Parkhurst associates with this word, the Greek *Phemi*—to speak, so perhaps another form of title may be Phemander—one who spoke to man.

There are two other persons mentioned in the *Pymander*; these are Tat assumed to be a son of Hermes, and Asclepius a grandson.

The *Pymander* has been many times printed, but it is a very difficult volume to obtain. Recent editions have been those of Hargrave Jennings, 1884, a reprint of Everard's English version; John David Chambers, Edinburgh, 1882, a new translation from the Greek; and that of L. Ménard, Paris, 1867.

Of earlier date are the Greek text of C. Parthey Berolins, 1854; an Italian version by C. Lenzoni, 1548; a German edition by J. Scheible, 1855; a French translation, François de Fois, 1579. The earliest Latin edition is that of Marsilius Ficinus, 1471, followed by Franciscus Patricius, 1593; Flussas, 1574; H. Rosselus, 1630; and 1676; and others contained in volumes associated with the writings of Lucius Apuleius of Madaura, and with the books attributed to Jamblichus of Chalcis.

The present edition is a *facsimile* reprint of the translation of the Rev. Dr. Everard from an Arabic text, of which there were two editions published in 1650 and 1657 respectively; this edition is from the earlier one. No alteration has been made except in the mode of spelling of a few words, the archaic form of which in the original would, it was feared, distract the reader's attention from the subject. It is preceded by a Preface by J.F., whose name is unknown. The second edition was a reprint of the *Pymander*, and contained in addition an English translation of fifteen chapters of *Asclepius* with a commentary.

Very little is known of the Rev. John Everard, D.D., but Alsager Vian states that he was born about 1575 and died about 1650. He entered the Church and remained a minister for many years, but was frequently suspended, sometimes for heretical doctrines and at others on account of political sermons. It is most probable that he was in truth a Neo-Platonist at heart and was also a disciple of the German mystic Tauler. His original works contain many quotations from Plato, Proclus and Plotinus.

With these notes I leave this Preface, without any attempt to comment on or explain the subject matter of the Pymander, believing that it will be better for a student to read and assimilate what he can from the original, rather than to read the work through my spectacles, or those of any other fellow student.

Should the present volume be found to supply a want, the remaining tracts attributed to Hermes will be reproduced in a succeeding volume of this series of "Collectanea Hermetica".

W. WYNN WESTCOTT.

"Palmam qui meruit ferat."

The Universe: the Twenty-First Key
of the Correct Tarot, (1884).

# INTRODUCTION[1]

TO THE

# "DIVINE PYMANDER."

---

THE Greeks applied the name and term of Hermes Mercurius Trismegistus, so significant and suggestive, certainly to the Egyptian Thoth, as early as the fourth century, B.C. He was believed to be the origin of everything formed or produced by the human mind. He was, therefore, esteemed as the inventor of all the arts and sciences. He was the contriver of the hieroglyphics. Of these there were various kinds. There was a profound system of hieroglyphical rendering, adopted among the Egyptians, the true meaning of which was only known to the higher ranks of the priests. There were other systems of representation by marks or figures which were less reserved, and some of these mysterious signs were fitted, or adapted, for the comprehension of the multitude. Hermes was the prolific and versatile interpreter between nature and man; the repository from which issued all the application of the methods of explaining the phenomena of nature and their uses, perceived by the human mind. In his hands, and through his means, lay the demonstration of the conclusions of reason.

The epithet, Trismegistus (ότρισμεγιστος, or "superlatively" greatest), as applied to Hermes, is of comparatively late origin, and cannot be traced to any author earlier than the second Christian century. Most probably, it arose out of the earlier forms derived by the Greeks from pristine Egyptian sources. But various other explanations of the appellation have been offered, such as that of the author of the *"Chronicon Alexandrinum"* (47 A.D.), who maintains that it was because Hermes, while maintaining the unity of God, had also asserted the existence of three supreme or greatest powers, that he was called by the Egyptians Trismegistus. This view, which is also adopted by Suidas, seems preferable at least to that met with in Nicolai's *"History of Greek Literature,"* according to which an apocryphal author named Hermes was called τρισμεγιστιος, simply in order to indicate that he had succeeded and outdone a certain Megistias of Smyrna in astrological, physiognomical, and alchemistic theories. The name of Hermes seems during the third and following centuries to have been regarded as a convenient pseudonym to place at the head of the numerous syncretistic writings in which it was sought to combine Neo-Platonic philosophy, Philonic Judaism, and Kabbalistic theosophy, and so provide the world with some acceptable substitute for the Christianity which had even at that time begun to give indications of the ascendancy it was destined afterwards to attain. Of these pseudepigraphic Hermetic writings, some have come down to us in the original Greek. Others survive in Latin or Arabic translations. But the majority appear to have perished.

That portion of the writings ascribed to Hermes Trismegistus which is best known, and which is most beyond dispute, forms, in its translation, the greater part of the present edition.[2] It bears its own expressions of excellence and authority, in that it is not only vividly written, but that it was the work of the most learnedly accomplished man of his age—Dr. Everard. A rich addition to the present publication, in regard to which work the great pains taken with it are evident, is the important illustration, "The Twenty-First Key of the Correct Tarot." Along with the above enumerated works of Hermes Trismegistus are usually printed the certainly later Ωροι, or

*Definitions* of Asclepius, which have sometimes but erroneously
been attributed to Apuleius. Other Hermetic writings, which
have been preserved, and which have been for the most part
collected by Patricius in the *"Nova de Universis Philosophia"*
(1593) are (in Latin) *"Aphorismi sive Centiloquium Cyranides"*; (in
Arabic, but doubtless from a Greek original), an address to the
human soul, which has been translated by Heischer, *"An die
menschliche Seele,"* 1870.

The connection of the name of Hermes with alchemy will
explain what is meant by "hermetic sealing," and will account
for the use of the phrase, "hermetic medicine" by Paracelsus,
as also for the so-called "Hermetic Freemasonry" of the
Middle Ages.

Hermes was called by the Egyptians TAT, TAUT, THOTH.
It is concluded that, because of his learning and address,
and in wonder at his profound skill in the arts and sciences,
that the people gave him the name of TRISMEGISTUS, or the
"THRICE GREAT." Thoth—or the being named with these
varieties of appellation, Tat, Tot, Taut, Thoth—was the
counsellor and friend of Osiris. This much has been declared
of him by Diodorus Siculus. He was left by Osiris to assist
Isis with his counsels in the government of the country, when
Osiris embarked in the design of regenerating the earth, and
visiting and civilizing the several nations. The historian adds
that Hermes improved language, invented letters, instituted
religious rites, taught mankind a consistent and philosophical
knowledge of Providence, instructed in astronomy, music,
and other arts. Many are of opinion that this Thoth, or
Hermes, lived long before the time of Moses. Some have
been so fanciful as to make him one with ADAM, while nearly
all historiographers, in surrounding his character and doings
with mystery, ascribe to him the power of magic, if not the very
invention of magic itself. There have not been wanting those
who have looked upon him as the same person as ENOCH or

CANAAN, or as the patriarch JOSEPH. Perhaps—in spite of all the foregoing exaggerations, which are always the lot of very great and highly distinguished men, who became deified in after-times—the most probable judgment to be formed concerning him is, that he was some person of superior genius, who, before the time of Moses, had invented useful arts, and taught the first rudiments of science; and who caused his instructions to be engraved in emblematical figures (hieroglyphics), upon tables or columns of stone (obelisks), which he dispersed over the country, for the purpose of enlightening the people, and of fixing the worship of the gods. And it is reasonable to conclude that the same symbolical inscriptions were made use of in calling up and inspiring the awe inseparable from the contemplation of spiritual beings—the guardians of the lives of men, and the disposers of their fates. Maxims of political and moral wisdom went hand in hand with these religious teachings.

Another Thoth, or Hermes, is said to have lived at a later period. He was equally celebrated with the former, and to him is particularly appropriated, by some, the name of Trismegistus. According to Manetho, he translated from engraved tables of stone, which had been buried in the earth, the sacred characters of the first Hermes, and wrote the explanation of them in books, which Were deposited in the Egyptian temples. The same author calls him the son of Agathodæmon; and adds, that to him are ascribed the restoration of the wisdom taught by the first Hermes, and the revival of geometry, arithmetic, and the arts, among the Egyptians, after they had been long lost or neglected. By the interpretation which he gave of the symbols inscribed upon the ancient tables or columns, he obtained the sanction of antiquity to his own institutions. To perpetuate their influence upon the minds of the people, he committed the columns, with his own interpretation, to the care of the priesthood. Hence, he obtained a high degree of respect among the people, and was long revered as the restorer of learning and the arts. He is said to have written a very large number of books, as commentaries upon the tables of the first Hermes, which treated of universal principles, of the nature of the universe, and of the soul of man; of the governing of the world by the movements of the stars (otherwise in astrology); of the Divine light, and of its shadow, or of its OTHER SIDE (presented away), in the MORTAL LIFE, or of the articulate breath or inspiration, or *means of being in this world*—which, in contradistinction to the life of the unbodied light, is the DARKNESS. All these ultra-profound ideas were treated of in the theosophical teaching (strictly Platonic, as it afterwards became) of HERMES, the "THRICE GREAT." He discourses of the nature and orders of the celestial beings; the populace of the elements; and herein he enunciates all the Kabbalistic notions of the ROSICRUCIANS. He reduces astrology to a system; he produces treatises on medicine; and enlarges, in a brilliant and inspired manner, on all the positive and recognisable side of anatomy, and also upon the mysticism connected with the origin and working of the world, and of the nature of the life of MAN. Clemens of Alexandria gives an account of his having written thirty-two books upon theology and philosophy, and six upon medicine, and mentions the particular subjects of some of them; but they are no longer in existence. The two dialogues which have been attributed to him, one of which is in the present reproduction, and the other (Asclepius, also numbered in the present work)—"Pymander" and "Asclepius "—so known from the names of the principal speakers in them, are most striking and eloquent. They give eloquent proof of the greatness of the author, real or supposed. But we are inclined to the opinion that he was a real being, supernaturally gifted; and thus offering to the world two characters—the one human, the other spiritual and divine.

The titles appropriated to HERMES MERCURIUS TRISMEGISTUS were, in part, the titles of the DEITY. THEUTH, THOTH, TAUT,

TAANTES, are the same title diversified, and they belong to the chief god of Egypt. Eusebius speaks of him as the same as HERMES. From Theuth the Greeks formed ΘΕΟΣ, or Theos, which with that nation was the most general name of the Deity. Plato, in his treatise named "Philebus," mentions him by the name of Θευθ, or Theuth. He was looked upon as a great benefactor, and the first cultivator of the vine. He was also supposed to have found out letters, which invention is likewise attributed to Hermes. Suidas calls him Theus, and says that he was the same as Arez, and so worshipped at Petra. Instead of a statue there was, "Lithos melas, tetragonos, atupōtos," a black square pillar of stone, without any figure or representation. It was the same deity which the Germans and Celtæ worshipped under the name of Theut-Ait or Theutates; whose sacrifices were very cruel, as we learn from Lucan:—

"Et quibus immitis placatur sanguine diro Theutates."[3]

*Lucan I*, v. 444.

The Hermetic or Hermetical art is a name given to chemistry, on the supposition that HERMES TRISMEGISTUS was the inventor of chemistry, or that he excelled in it. Very little is known, indeed, of this Hermes, and still less of how much or how little he had to do with the invention of the art of chemistry. He is reputed to be an ancient king of Egypt by some who have endeavoured to trace his history. The era of Æsculapius is ancient enough, but these explorers will insist that the age of HERMES TRISMEGISTUS far preceded it. These assign his time to a thousand years before the period of Æsculapius. They carry HERMES TRISMEGISTUS into perfect mystery. Zozimus Panopolity mentions him as having wrote of natural things, and there are many pieces existent under his name which are certainly—to speak the least of them—under some doubt.

The numerous books upon theology, astronomy, and medicine are ascribed by Marsham (in *Chronicle* s.l) to the second Mercury, the Son of Vulcan, who, according to Eusebius (in *Chronicle*) lived a little after Moses; that is, about fifty years after the exodus of the Israelites. This learned author, relying upon the authority of Manetho, cited by Cincellus, reckons that this second Mercury is he who was surnamed "Trismegistus," or "Thrice Great." According to Manetho, this second Hermes or Mercury translated from engraved tables of stone, that had been hidden in the earth, the sacred characters written by the first Hermes or Mercury, called Thaut or Thoth, and wrote the explanation in books, which were deposited in the Egyptian temples. He thus established a Divine authority, obtained a high degree of respect among the people, and was long revered as the restorer of learning. From the tables of the first Hermes he is said to have written, as commentaries and explanations, an incredible number of books. These books, according to Clemens Alexandrinus (*Strom.* i. 6) amounted in number to forty-two. It was impossible for the Egyptians to carry their veneration for them higher than they did. They were borne in their processions with great ceremony and respect. First of all appeared the "Chanter," who had two of them in his hands, one containing the hymns in honour of the gods, and the other rules according to which the kings were to govern. Next came the "Horoscopus," or that minister, as Clemens informs us, who carried the four books of astronomy: one treating of the fixed stars, another of the eclipses of the sun and moon, and the two last of the rising of these two luminaries. Then appeared the sacred "Scribe," with ten books that treated of cosmography, geography, the description of the Nile, *etc.* Then followed the "Stolist," with other ten books, on the subject of religion, namely, sacrifices, prayers, festival days, *etc.* The "Prophet" came next, with ten books, which were named sacerdotal, and treated of the laws of the gods, and of ecclesiastical discipline.

"Thus," says the author now cited, "there were forty-two books in all, of which thirty-six comprehended all that belonged to the Egyptian philosophy. The other six books regarded medicine, and treated of anatomy, medicaments, diseases of the eyes, of women, and of regulations to be practised in domestic association. These books—at all events, in any number—long ago lost, if any answering the above descriptions ever existed, at least in the manner stated of them, furnished Sanchoniathon with the materials for his theogony. Many subjects on which these writings are said to have treated are generally supposed to have been unknown in the early period of the Egyptian philosophy.

If we consult alchemical manuscripts, no matter the date or author or language, we find constant mention of HERMES TRISMEGISTUS, who was indeed considered, and sometimes designated, the father of *Alchemy*. In a treatise attributed to Albertus Magnus, we are told that the tomb of HERMES was discovered by Alexander the Great in a cave near Hebron. In this was found a slab of emerald, which had been taken, from the hands of the dead Hermes, by "Sarah, the wife of Abraham," and which had inscribed upon it, in Phœnician characters, the precepts of the great master concerning the art of making gold. The inscription consisted of thirteen sentences, and is to be found in numerous alchemical works. It is for the most part very difficult to be understood, and in this respect closely resembles most of the great mass of the Middle-Age alchemical literature.

The following is cited as the inscription of the "Smaragdine Table," and is to be found in very early MSS. In various languages:—

Firstly:—I speak not fictitious things, but that which is certain and most true.

Secondly:—What is below, is like that which is above; and what is above, is like that which is below: to accomplish the miracle of one thing.

Thirdly:—And as all things were produced by the one word of one Being, so all things were produced from this one thing by adaptation.

Fourthly:—Its father is the sun, its mother the moon, the wind carries it in its belly, its nurse is the earth.

Fifthly:—It is the father of all perfection throughout the world.

Sixthly:—The power is vigorous if it be changed into earth.

Seventhly:—Separate the earth from the fire, the subtle from the gross, acting prudently and with judgment.

Eighthly:—*Ascend* with the greatest sagacity from the earth to heaven, and then again *descend* to the earth, and *unite together* the *powers of things superior and things inferior*. Thus, you will obtain the *glory* of the *whole world*, and obscurity will fly away from you.

Ninthly:—This has more fortitude than fortitude itself, because it conquers every subtle thing, and can penetrate every solid.

Tenthly:—Thus was the world formed.

Eleventhly:—Hence proceed wonders which are here established.

Twelfthly:—Therefore I am called HERMES TRISMEGISTUS, having three parts of the philosophy of the whole world.

Thirteenthly:—That which I had to say concerning the operation of the sun is completed.

The story and the inscription, together with all books attributed to Hermes (who is asserted to have lived about 2,000 B.C.) are still matter of dispute (occasionally vehement) among the learned. In spite of the obvious difficulty of interpretation of the inscription of the "Emerald Table," men (and men of extraordinary capacity) have not been wanting who have laboured long and lovingly to prove its authenticity, to interpret it, and to show that it is, in good sooth, a marvellous revelation, full of sublime secrets of considerable import to mankind.

HERMES TRISMEGISTUS is generally asserted by the alchemists to have been a priest, who lived a little after the time of Moses. According to Clemens Alexandrinus, he was the author of forty-two books, containing all the learning of the Egyptians. Others tell us that he was the author of several thousand volumes. Plato speaks of him in the Phædrus as the inventor of numbers and letters. He was, in fact, the Egyptian god of letters, and as such, of course, could be described as the author of multitudinous works. He was the deified intellect, and hence has often been confounded with THOTH, the "intellect." Sir Gardner Wilkinson speaks of HERMES as an emanation of THOTH, and as representing the "abstract quality" of the understanding. It may be well to note the extent of the symbolism associated with the sculptured representations, and with the hieroglyphics associated with the name of HERMES TRISMEGISTUS. In one hand Hermes holds the *crux ansata,* the symbol of life—a master symbol which is the most persistent and determined in its appearance (and in its re-appearance) in all the sculptures of Egypt:—in the other hand the figure grasps a staff, associated with which are a serpent, a scorpion, a hawk's head, and above all a circle surrounded by an asp, each with its special symbolical significance. On the Rosetta stone Hermes is called the "great and great," or "twice" great. He was called TRISMEGISTUS, or "thrice great," according to the twelfth aphorism of the Emerald Table, because he possessed *three parts* of the wisdom of the whole world.

Perhaps no author is more often quoted by the alchemists than Hermes, the supposed father of their art. They called themselves Hermetic philosophers. Alchemy is often called the "Hermetic Art," or simply "Hermetics." To enclose a substance very securely, as by placing it in a glass tube and fusing or sealing the mouth of the tube, was called securing with "Hermes, his seal," and the echo of the idea lives amongst us yet, for, in our most modern treatises, the expression to "seal hermetically" may be found.

Colonel Franklin (p. 5.) says:—

> The learned Maurice entertains no doubt that the elder Boodh of India is no other than the elder Hermes Trismegistus of Egypt, and that that original character is of antidiluvian race. Here then is an analogy amounting almost too positive and irrefragable conviction; for Boodh and Jeyne are known throughout Hindostan, with very little exception, to be one and the same personage.

In p. 41, Colonel Franklin remarks that Bacchus agrees in his attributes with the Indian Boodh. And Mr. Faber observes "that Thor is represented as the first-born of the Supreme God, and is styled in the Edda 'the eldest of Sons.' " (Faber, *Horæ Mosaicæ*, Vol. I.) "He was esteemed in Scandinavia as a middle divinity, *a mediator* between God and man."— (Franklin's *Res.*, p. 49.) "Brahma is generally in the neuter gender; but as Vishnu or Naragen he is masculine, as he is also when he is considered as the Creator." (Asiat. *Res.*, Vol. I., pp. 242, 243; Collier, Sect. IV.)

Buddha in Egypt was called Hermes Trismegistus. Lycophron calls him *Tricephalus;* this speaks for itself, as we are aware that Buddha is identified with Brahma, Vishnu, and Siva.

The T, Tau, was the instrument of death, but it was also what Ezekiel ordered the people in Jerusalem to be marked with, who were to be *saved from the destroyer.* It was also the emblem of the Taranis or the Thoth, or Teutates, or Tat, or Hermes, or Buddha among the Druids. It was called the *Crux Hermis.* The old Hebrew, the Bastulan, and the Pelasgian, have the letter Tau thus:— X; the Etruscan, + X; the Coptic, +; the Punic, ϽϹ ϽϹ.

The opposition which the possibility of the powers of nature, acting in the conversion of the baser metals into gold, evokes from the supposed learned modern people—with whom we confess we are at utter issue—is remarkable, and indeed inexcusable, when the wonders (once thought unbelievable), which are almost daily witnessed, recur to the remembrance. *Perhaps no age was so incredulously fixed in its own prepossessions as the present.* We will conclude our essay on the character and claims of the person known to the world as HERMES MERCURIUS TRISMEGISTUS, with an account by a modern scientific man, which seems almost *spiteful* in its ignorant attack upon a philosopher of the most undoubted original genius, whose book, in Italian, "*De Cabinetto*" (or "Gabinetto"), is considered by all competent people who have examined the deepest into these very mysterious subjects—in companionship with the true edition of the allegory entitled the "*Comte de Gabalis*" of the Abbé de Villars,[4] as supplying an outline, veiled in the proper mysterious terms, of the profound system of the *true* Rosicrucians. The reader may note (with displeasure) the perverse ingenuity with which this author endeavours to invest with ridicule that which he may be safely accepted as incompetent to understand.

"Petrus Hauboldus, of Copenhagen, was surely one of the most enterprising publishers of his day, for he had the temerity to publish a book entitled '*Hermetes Ægyptiorum et Chemichorum Sapientia.*' A book square as to its dimensions, small as to its type, drier than dust as to its contents, of four hundred odd pages, of two centuries of age, written in Latin, with a sprinkling of contracted Greek, and floridly dedicated to Jean Baptiste Colbert. A book wherein the author endeavours to prove that alchemy was known before the flood, that Hermes Trismegistus was a real personage, the inventor of all arts, the father of alchemy, and much else besides. We may well imagine that the author of such a treatise was no ordinary man, and our conjecture proves a tolerably correct one. Olaf Borch, whose Latinised name became the more resounding *Olaus Borrichius,* was apparently the great mainstay of the University of Copenhagen; at all events, he was simultaneously Professor of

Philology, Poetry, Chemistry, and Botany; and we must either imagine that, in 1660, professors were difficult to procure in the Kingdom of Denmark, or else that Olaus Borrichius was such an astounding genius that he could readily undertake the duties of four diverse professorships at the same time. We can scarcely imagine three greater antitheses than the philological faculty, the poetical faculty, and the chemical faculty; but here we find them united, or assumed to be united, in one man. Yet more, Borrichius was appointed Court Physician, and Assessor of the Supreme Court of Law. He was the very personification of all learning, if we may judge by the treatment he received from his countrymen. In addition to the work mentioned above, he wrote various treatises on philology, on the quantity of syllables, on the Greek and Latin poets, on medicine, chemistry, and botany. It is strange that a man who, presumably in his capacity of judge, was in the habit of sifting evidence, and of avoiding hasty generalisation, should have endeavoured with much elaborate argument to prove that Hermes Trismegistus was a real personage; that his *Smaragdine Table* was really found by the wife of Abraham, and that it contained matter of the highest import to mankind. We must imagine that in this matter Borrichius allowed the imaginative faculty due to his poetical temperament to exert an undue influence over his more sober judgment. He is equally at pains to assert the authenticity and antiquity of the various Greek MSS. on alchemy in the libraries of Europe. He specially mentions a MS. by Zozimus of Panapolis, on the art of making gold, in the King's Library in Paris; and Scaliger tells us that this same MS. was written in the fifth century. M. Ferdinand Hoefer is apparently penetrated by the Borrichian spirit of faith and imagination, and he unhesitatingly accepts the early date attributed to the Paris MS."

HARGRAVE JENNINGS, 1884.

Notes:

1. It is to be remarked that the Preface and Preliminary Essay by the distinguished author of the *"Rosicrucians," "Phallicism," etc.,* "Hargrave Jennings," first intimated as distinct, are presented combined in his exhaustive, scholarly *resumé* as the most suitable form of Introduction to this DOUBLE ENTENTE Work, which is also said still to exist symbolically in that most extraordinary Ancient combination of Hieroglyphics, Metaphysics, and Mathematics that ever occupied the attention of the human mind, indicated by "Guillaume Postel" in his "Key of Things Concealed since the Commencement of the World," and known only to Initiates.—R.H.F.

2. And also of his *"Virgin of the World,"* now being translated, and shortly to be issued as the companion volume to, and uniform in size with the present work.—R.H.F.

3. "And they appeased Theutates with the use of cursed and dreadful blood."—D.K.

4. An early facsimile edition of *"Comte de Gabalis"* of the Abbé de Villars was printed by Robert H. Fryer, Bath, 1886.—D.K.

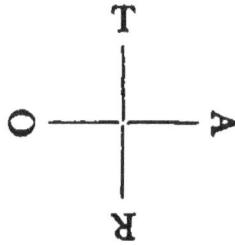

T
O —|— A
R

# TO THE READER[1]

# "DIVINE PYMANDER."

———

Judicious Reader,

THIS Book may justly challenge the first place for antiquity, from all the Books in the World, being written some hundreds of years before *Moses'* time, as I shall endeavour to make good. The Original (as far as is known to us) is *Arabic*, and several Translations thereof have been published, as *Greek, Latin, French, Dutch, etc.*, but never *English* before. It is pity the Learned Translator[2] had not lived, and received himself, the honour, and thanks due to him from the *Englishmen*; for his good will to, and pains for them, in translating a Book of such infinite worth, out of the Original, into their Mother-tongue.

Concerning the Author of the Book itself, Four things are considerable, *viz.*, His Name, Learning, Country, and Time.

1. The name by which he was commonly styled, is *Hermes Trismegistus, i.e., Mercurius ter Maximus*, or, The thrice greatest Intelligencer. And well might he be called *Hermes*, for he was the first Intelligencer in the World (as we read of) that communicated Knowledge to the sons of Men, by Writing, or Engraving. He was called *Ter Maximus*, for some Reasons, which I shall afterwards mention.

2. His Learning will appear, as by his Works; so by the right understanding the Reason of his Name.

3. For his Country, he was King of Egypt.

4. For his Time, it is not without much Controversy, betwixt those that write of this Divine, ancient Author, what time he lived in. Some say he lived after *Moses* his time, giving this slender Reason for it, *viz.*, Because he was named *Ter Maximus*: for being preferred[3] (according to the *Egyptian Customs*) being chief Philosopher, to be chief of the Priesthood: and from thence, to be chief in Government, or King. But if this be all their ground, you must excuse my dissent from them, and that for this reason, Because according to the most learned of his followers,[4] he was called *Ter Maximus*; for having perfect, and exact Knowledge of all things contained in the World; which things he divided into Three Kingdoms (as he calls them), *viz.*, *Mineral, Vegetable, Animal;* which Three, he did excel in the right understanding of; also, because he attained to, and transmitted to Posterity (although in an Ænigmatical, and obscure style) the Knowledge of the Quintessence of the whole Universe (which Universe, as I said before, he divided into Three Parts) otherwise called, The great *Elixir* of the Philosophers; which is the Receptacle of all Celestial and Terrestrial Virtues; which Secret, many ignorantly deny, many have chargeably sought after, yet few, but some, yea, and the *Englishmen*[5] have happily found. The Description of this great Treasure, is said to be found engraved upon a *Smaragdine* Table, in the Valley of *Ebron*, after the Flood. So that the Reason before alleged to prove this Author to live after *Moses*, seem invalid: neither doth it any way appear, that he lived in *Moses* his time, although it be the opinion of some, as of *John Functius*, who saith in his Chronology, That he lived Twenty-one years before the *Law* was given by *Moses* in the Wilderness; But the Reasons that he, and others give, are far weaker than those that I shall give, for his living before *Moses* his time. My reasons for that are these:—

First, Because it is received amongst the Ancients, that he was the first that invented the Art of communicating Knowledge to the World, by Writing or Engraving. Now if so, then in all probability he was before *Moses*; for it is said of *Moses*, that he was from his childhood,[6] skilled in all the *Egyptian* Learning, which could not well have been without the help of Literature, which we never read of any before that invented by *Hermes*.

Secondly, he is said by himself, to be the son of *Saturn*,[7] and by others to be the Scribe of *Saturn*.[8] Now *Saturn* according to Historians, lived in the time of *Sarug, Abraham's* great Grand-Father. I shall but take in *Suidas* his judgment, and so rest satisfied, that he did not live only before, but long before *Moses*; His words are these, *Credo Mercurium Trismegistum sapientem Egyptium floruisse ante Pharaonem*.[9]

In this Book, though so very old, is contained more true knowledge of God and Nature, than in all the Books in the World besides, I except only Sacred Writ; And they that shall judiciously read it, and rightly understand it, may well be excused from reading many Books; the Authors of which, pretend so much to the knowledge of the Creator, and Creation. If God ever appeared in any man, he appeared in him, as it appears by this Book. That a man who had not the benefit of his Ancestors' knowledge, being as I said before, The first inventor of the Art of Communicating Knowledge to Posterity by writing, should be so high a Divine, and so deep a Philosopher, seems to be a thing more of God than of Man; and therefore it was the opinion of some,[10] That he came from Heaven, not born upon Earth. There is contained in this Book, that true Philosophy, without which, it is impossible ever to attain to the height, and exactness of Piety, and Religion. According to this Philosophy, I call him a Philosopher, that shall learn and study the things that are, and how they are ordered, and governed, and by whom, and for what cause, or to what end; and he that doth so, will acknowledge thanks to, and admire the Omnipotent Creator, Preserver, and Director of all these things. And he that shall be thus truly thankful, may truly be called Pious and Religious: and he that is Religious, shall more and more, know where, and what the Truth is: And learning that, he shall yet be more and more Religious.

The glory and splendour of Philosophy, is an endeavouring to understand the chief Good, as the Fountain of all Good: Now how can we come near to, or find out the Fountain, but by making use of the Streams as a conduct to it? The operations of Nature, are Streams running from the Fountain of Good, which is God. I am not of the ignorant, and foolish opinion of those that say, The greatest Philosophers are the greatest Atheists: as if to know the works of God, and to understand his goings forth in the Way of Nature, must necessitate a man to deny God. The Scripture [11] disapproves of this as a sottish tenet, and experience contradicts it: For behold! Here is the greatest Philosopher, and therefore the greatest Divine.

Read understandingly this ensuing Book (and for thy help thou mayest make use of that voluminous Commentary written upon it) [12] then it will speak more for its Author, than can be spoken by any man, at least by me.

Thine in the love

of Truth,

J.F.

Notes:
1. To the Reader of the "Divine Pymander" was the original preface to the 1650 edition by J.F.—D.K.
2. Revd. Dr. John Everard.
3. Franciscus Flussas.
4. Geber Paratel, Paracelsus; Henricus Nollius in *Theoria Philosophiæ Hermeticæ, tractatu primo.*
5. Ripley, Bacon, Norton, *etc.*
6. Acts vii; 22.
7. Chapter X.

8. Sanchoniathon.
9. Suidas' [words translate as "I believe Mercury Trismegistus was the wisest man to have flourished before the Egyptian Pharaohs.—D.K.]
10. Goropius Becanus.
11. Job xxxviii.
12. The author's name used for the Robert H. Fryar 1884 edition and the Westcott 1894 edition was "Hanbal Offeli Alabar." The most recognized spelling of the author's name is "Hannibal Rosseli Calabari." His extensive commentary was printed in the book, *Pymander Mercurii Trismegisti*. It was written in Latin and printed at Cracow by Lazarus in six volumes from 1585 to 1590. It was later reprinted in Cologne in 1630 and titled *Divinus Pimander Hermetis Mercurii Trismegisti*.—D.K.

# PYMANDER
## MERCVRII
### TRISMEGISTI.

*Cum Commento*

FRATRIS HANNIBALIS ROSSELI
CALABRI ORDINIS MINORVM REGVLARIS
*obſeruantiæ, Theologiæ & Philoſophiæ, ad*
*S. Bernardinum Cracouiæ*
*Profeſſoris.*

## Liber primus de SS. Trinitate.

*Cum licentia & authoritate Illuſtriſſimi & Reuerendiſſ. Domini Alberti*
*Bologneti Cardinalis, & in Regno Poloniæ Nuntij Apoſtolici.*

Cumq́; Gratia & Priuilegio Sacræ Cæſareæ M.
& Sereniſſ. Regis Poloniæ.

## CRACOVIAE.
### In Officina Typographica Lazari: Anno
## M. D. LXXXV.

Title page for *Pymander Mercurii Trismegisti* (1585).

THE

# DIVINE PYMANDER

OF

# HERMES MERCURIUS TRISMEGISTUS

## IN XVII. BOOKS

Translated formerly out of the *Arabick* into *Greek*, and thence into *Latine*, and *Dutch*, and now out of the Original into *English;*

By that Learned Divine

## DOCTOR EVERARD

*London.* Printed by Robert White, for Thos. Brewster and Greg. Moule, at the Three Bibles in the Poultrey, under Mildreds Church, 1650.

*The Divine Pymander* was first published in 1894 by Theosophical Publishing Society, London as part of the *Collectanea Hermetica* series.

This edition was published by The Golden Dawn Research Trust in 2012.

# The Titles of every Book
## of
# Hermes Trismegistus.

——•••◉•••——

# The Divine Pymander.

"HERMES TRISMEGISTUS,"

THE FIRST BOOK.

I, O my Son, write this First Book, both for Humanity's sake, and for Piety towards God.

2. For there can be no Religion more true or just, than to know the things that are; and to acknowledge thanks for all things, to Him that made them, which thing I shall not cease continually to do.

3. What then should a man do, O Father, to lead his life well; seeing there is nothing here true?

4. Be Pious and Religious, O my Son; for he that doth so, is the best and highest Philosopher; and without Philosophy, it is impossible ever to attain to the height and exactness of Piety or Religion.

5. But he that shall learn and study the things that are, and how they are ordered and governed, and by whom, and for what cause, or to what end, will acknowledge thanks to the *Workman*, as to a good *Father*, an excellent *Nurse*, and a faithful *Steward*, and he that gives thanks shall be Pious or Religious, and he that is Religious shall know both where the truth is, and what it is, and learning that he will be yet more and more Religious.

6. For never, O Son, shall or can that Soul, which, while it is in the Body lightens and lifts up itself to know and comprehend that which is Good and True, slide back to the contrary; for it is infinitely enamoured thereof, and forgetteth all Evils; and when it hath learned and known its *Father* and *Progenitor*, it can no more Apostatize or depart from that Good.

7. And let this, O Son, be the end of Religion and Piety; whereunto thou art once arrived, thou shalt both live well, and die blessedly, whilst thy Soul is not ignorant whether it must return, and fly back again.

8. For this only, O Son, is the way to *Truth*, which our *Progenitors* travelled in; and by which, making their journey, they at length attained to the Good. It is a Venerable way and plain, but hard and difficult for the Soul to go in that is in the Body.

9. For first must it war against its own self, and after much Strife and Dissention, it must be overcome of one part; for the Contention is of one against two, whilst it flies away, and they strive to hold and detain it.

10. But the victory of both is not like, for the one hasteth to that which is Good, but the other is a neighbour to the things that are Evil; and that which is Good, desireth to be set at liberty; but the things that are Evil, love Bondage and Slavery.

11. And if the two parts be overcome, they become quiet, and are content to accept of it as their *Ruler*; but if the one be overcome of the two, it is by them led and carried to be punished by its being and continuance here.

12. This is, O Son, the Guide in the way that leads thither; for thou must first forsake the Body before thy end, and get the victory in this Contention and Strifeful life, and when thou hast overcome, return.

13. But now, O my Son, I will by Heads run through the things that are: understand thou what I say, and remember what thou hearest.

14. All things that are moved; only that which is not, is unmoveable.

15. Every Body is changeable.

16. Not every Body is dissolvable.

17. Some bodies are dissolvable.

18. Every living being is not mortal.

19. Nor every living thing is immortal.

20. That which may be dissolved is also corruptible.

21. That which abides always is unchangeable.

22. That which is unchangeable is eternal.

23. That which is always made is always corrupted.

24. That which is made but once, is never corrupted, neither becomes any other thing.

25. Firstly, God; Secondly, the World; Thirdly, Man.

26. The World for Man, Man for God.

27. Of the Soul; that part which is Sensible is mortal, but that part which is Reasonable is immortal.

28. Every Essence is immortal.

29. Every Essence is unchangeable.

30. Everything that is, is double.

31. None of the things that are stand still.

32. Not all things are moved by a Soul, but everything that is, is moved by a Soul.

33. Everything that suffers is Sensible; everything that is Sensible suffereth.

34. Everything that is sad rejoiceth also, and is a mortal living Creature.

35. Not everything that joyeth is also sad, but is an eternal living thing.

36. Not every Body is sick; every Body that is sick is dissolvable.

37. The Mind in God.

38. Reasoning (or disputing or discoursing) in Man.

39. Reason in the Mind.

40. The Mind is void of suffering.

41. No thing in a Body true.

42. All that is incorporeal, is void of Lying.

43. Everything that is made is corruptible.

44. Nothing good upon Earth; nothing evil in Heaven.

45. God is good; Man is evil.

46. Good is voluntary, or of its own accord.

47. Evil is involuntary, or against its will.

48. The Gods choose good things, as good things.

49. Time is a Divine thing.

50. Law is Humane.

51. Malice is the nourishment of the World.

52. Time is the corruption of Man.

53. Whatsoever is in Heaven is unalterable.

54. All upon Earth is alterable.

55. Nothing in Heaven is servanted, nothing upon Earth free.

56. Nothing unknown in Heaven, nothing known upon Earth.

57. The things upon Earth communicate not with those in Heaven.

58. All things in Heaven are unblameable, all things upon Earth are subject to Reprehension.

59. That which is immortal, is not mortal: that which is mortal is not immortal.

60. That which is sown, is not always begotten; but that which is begotten always, is sown.

61. Of a dissolveable Body, there are two Times, one for sowing to generation, one from generation to death.

62. Of an everlasting Body, the time is only from the Generation.

63. Dissolveable Bodies are increased and diminished.

64. Dissolveable matter is altered into contraries; to wit, Corruption and Generation, but Eternal matter into its self, and its like.

65. The Generation of Man is Corruption; the Corruption of Man is the beginning of Generation.

66. That which off-springs or begetteth another, is itself an offspring or begotten by another.

67. Of things that are, some are in Bodies, some in their *Ideas*.

68. Whatsoever things belong to operation or working, are in a Body.

69. That which is immortal, partakes not of that which is mortal.

70. That which is mortal, cometh not into a Body immortal, but that which is immortal, cometh into that which is mortal.

71. Operation or Workings are not carried upwards, but descend downwards.

72. Things upon Earth do nothing to advantage those in Heaven, but all things in Heaven do profit and advantage all things upon Earth.

73. Heaven is capable, and a fit receptacle of everlasting Bodies, the Earth of corruptible Bodies.

74. The Earth is brutish, the Heaven is reasonable or rational.

75. Those things that are in Heaven are subjected or placed under it, but the things on Earth, are placed upon it.

76. Heaven is the first Element.

77. Providence is Divine Order.

78. Necessity is the Minister or Servant of Providence.

79. Fortune is the carriage or effect of that which is without Order; the Idol of operation, a lying Fantasy or opinion.

80. What is God? The immutable or unalterable Good.

81. What is man? An unchangeable Evil.

82. If thou perfectly remember these Heads, thou canst not forget those things which in more words I have largely expounded unto thee; for these are the Contents or Abridgment of them.

83. Avoid all Conversation with the multitude or common People; for I would not have thee subject to Envy, much less to be ridiculous unto the many.

84. For the like always takes to itself that which is like, but the unlike never agrees with the unlike: such Discourses as these have very few Auditors, and peradventure very few will have, but they have something peculiar unto themselves.

85. They do rather sharpen and whet evil men to their maliciousness, therefore it behoveth to avoid the multitude, and take heed of them as not understanding the virtue and power of the things that are said.

86. How dost thou mean, O Father?

87. Thus, O Son, the whole Nature and Composition of those living things called Men, is very prone to Maliciousness, and is very familiar, and as it were nourished with it, and therefore is delighted with it. Now this wight, if it shall come to learn or know, that the world was once made, and all things are done according to Providence or Necessity, Destiny or Fate, bearing Rule over all: Will he not be much worse than himself, despising the whole because it was made? And if he may lay the cause of Evil upon Fate or Destiny, he will never abstain from any evil work.

88. Wherefore we must look warily to such kind of people, that being in ignorance, they may be less evil for fear of that which is hidden and kept secret.

THE END OF

THE FIRST BOOK OF HERMES.

# THE SECOND BOOK,

CALLED

## "POEMANDER."

———

MY thoughts being once seriously busied about things that are, and my Understanding lifted up, all my bodily Senses being exceedingly holden back, as it is with them that are very heavy of sleep, by reason either of fulness of meat, or of bodily labour: Me thought I saw one of an exceeding great stature, and of an infinite greatness, call me by my name, and say unto me, "What wouldest thou Hear and See? Or what wouldst thou Understand, to Learn and Know?"

2. Then said I, "Who are Thou?" "I am," quoth he, "Poemander, the mind of the Great Lord, the most Mighty and absolute Emperor: I know what thou wouldst have, and I am always present with thee."

3. Then I said, "I would Learn the Things that are, and Understand the Nature of them, and know God." "How?" said he. I answered, "That I would gladly hear." Then said he, "Have me again in thy mind, and whatsoever though wouldst learn, I will teach thee."

4. When he had thus said, he was changed in his Idea or Form, and straightway, in the twinkling of an eye, all things were opened unto me: and I saw an infinite Sight, all things were become light, both sweet and exceeding pleasant; and I was wonderfully delighted in the beholding it.

5. But after a little while, there was a darkness made in part, coming down obliquely, fearful and hideous, which

seemed unto me to be changed into a Certain Moist Nature, unspeakably troubled, which yielded a smoke as from Fire; and from whence proceeded a voice unutterable, and very mournful, but inarticulate, insomuch as it seemed to have come from the Light.

6. Then from that Light, a certain Holy Word joined itself unto Nature, and out flew the pure and unmixed Fire from the moist Nature upwards on high; it was exceeding Light, and Sharp, and Operative withal. And the Air, which was also light, followed the Spirit and mounted up to Fire (from the Earth and the Water), insomuch that it seemed to hang and depend upon it.

7. And the Earth and the Water stayed by themselves so mingled together, that the Earth could not be seen for the Water, but they were moved, because of the Spiritual Word that was carried upon them.

8. Then said Poemander unto me, "Dost thou understand this Vision, and what it meaneth?" "I shall know," said I. Then said he, "I am that Light, the Mind, thy God, who am before that Moist Nature that appeareth out of Darkness; and that Bright and Lightful Word from the Mind is the Son of God."

9. "How is that?" quoth I. "Thus," replied he, "Understand it: That which in thee Seeth and Heareth, the Word of the Lord, and the Mind, the Father, God, Differeth not One from the Other, and the Unison of these is Life."

TRISMEGISTUS:—I thank thee. PIMANDER:—But first conceive well the Light in thy mind, and know it.

10. When he had thus said, for a long time we looked steadfastly one upon the other, insomuch that I trembled at his Idea or Form.

11. But when he nodded to me, I beheld in my mind the Light that is in innumerable, and the truly indefinite Ornament or World; and that the Fire is comprehended or contained in, or by a most great Power, and constrained to keep its station.

12. These things I understood, seeing the word of Pimander; and when I was mightily amazed, he said again unto me, "Hast thou seen in thy mind that Archetypal Form, which was before the Interminated and Infinite Beginning?" Thus Pimander to me. "But whence," quoth I, "or whereof are the Elements of Nature made?"

PIMANDER:—Of the Will and Counsel of God; which taking the Word, and beholding the beautiful World (in the Archetype thereof) imitated it, and so made this World, by the principles and vital Seeds or Soul-like productions of itself.

13. For the Mind being God, Male and Female, Life and Light, brought forth by his Word; another Mind or Workman: which being God of the Fire, and the Spirit, fashioned and formed seven other Governors, which in their Circles contain the Sensible World, whose Government or Disposition is called Fate or Destiny.

14. Straightway leaped out, or exalted itself from the downward born Elements of God, the Word of God, into the clean and pure Workmanship of Nature, and was united to the Workman, Mind, for it was Consubstantial; and so the downward born Elements of Nature were left without Reason, that they might be the only Matter.

15. But the Workman, Mind, together with the Word, containing the Circles, and Whirling them about, turned round as a Wheel, his own Workmanships, and suffered them to be turned from an indefinite Beginning to an undeterminable End; for they always begin where they end.

16. And the Circulation or running round of these, as the Mind willeth, out of the lower or downward-born Elements, brought forth unreasonable or brutish Creatures, for they had no reason, the Air flying things, and the Water such as swim.

17. And the Earth and the Water were separated, either from the other, as the Mind would: and the Earth brought forth

from herself, such Living Creatures as she had, four-footed and creeping beasts, wild and tame.

18. But the Father of all things, the Mind being Life and Light, brought forth Man like unto himself, whom he loved as his proper Birth, for he was all beauteous, having the image of his Father.

19. For indeed God was exceedingly enamoured of his own Form or Shape, and delivered unto it all his own Workmanships. But he seeing and understanding the Creation of the Workman in the whole, would needs also himself Fall to Work, and so was separated from the Father, being in the sphere of Generation or Operation.

20. Having all Power, he considered the Operations or Workmanships of the Seven; but they loved him, and everyone made him partaker of his own Order.

21. And he learning diligently, and understanding their Essence, and partaking their Nature, resolved to pierce and break through the Circumference of the Circles, and to understand the Power of him that sits upon the Fire.

22. And having already all power of mortal things, of the Living, and of the unreasonable Creatures of the World, stooped down and peeped through the Harmony, and breaking through the strength of the Circles, so shewed and made manifest the downward-born Nature, the fair and beautiful Shape or Form of God.

23. Which, when he saw, having in itself the unsatiable Beauty, and all the Operations of the Seven Governors, and the Form or Shape of God, he Smiled for love, as if he had seen the Shape or Likeness in the Water, or the shadow upon the Earth of the fairest Human form.

24. And seeing in the Water a shape, a shape like unto himself, in himself he loved it, and would cohabit with it; and immediately upon the resolution, ensued the Operation, and brought forth the unreasonable Image or Shape.

25. Nature presently laying hold of what it so much loved, did wholly wrap herself about it, and they were mingled, for they loved one another.

26. And from this cause, Man above all things that live upon Earth, is double; Mortal because of his Body, and Immortal, because of the substantial Man: For being Immortal, and having power of all things, he yet suffers mortal things, and such as are subject to Fate or Destiny.

27. And therefore being above all Harmony, he is made and become a servant to Harmony. And being Hermaphrodite, or Male and Female, and watchful, he is governed by and subjected to a Father, that is both Male and Female, and watchful.

28. After these things, I said: "Thou art my Mind, and I am in love with Reason."

29. Then said Pimander, "This is the Mystery that to this day is hidden, and kept secret; for Nature being mingled with Man brought forth a Wonder most wonderful; for he having the Nature of the Harmony of the Seven, from him whom I told thee, the Fire and the Spirit, Nature continued not, but forth with brought forth seven Men, all Males and Females, and sublime, or on high, according to the Natures of the Seven Governors."

30. "And after these things, O Pimander," quoth I, "I am now come into a great desire, and longing to hear, do not digress or run out."

31. But he said, "Keep silence, for I have not yet finished the first speech."

32. TRISMEGISTUS:—Behold, I am silent.

33. PIMANDER:—The Generation therefore of these Seven was after this manner, the Air being Feminine and the Water desirous of Copulation, took from the Fire its ripeness, and from the Aether Spirit; and so Nature produced Bodies after the Species and Shape of men.

34. And Man was made of Life and Light, into Soul and Mind; of Life the soul, of Light the Mind.

35. And so all the Members of the Sensible World, continued unto the period of the end, bearing rule, and generating.

36. Hear now the rest of that speech, thou so much desireth to hear.

37. When that Period was fulfilled, the bond of all things was loosed and untied by the Will of God; for all living Creatures being Hermaphroditical, or Male and Female, were loosed and untied together with Man; and so the Males were apart by themselves and the Females likewise.

38. And straightway God said to the Holy Word, Increase in Increasing, and Multiply in Multitude all you my Creatures and Workmanships. And let Him that is endued with Mind, know Himself to be Immortal; and that the cause of Death is the Love of the Body, and let Him Learn all Things that are.

39. When he had thus said, Providence by Fate of Harmony, made the mixtures, and established the Generations, and all things were multiplied according to their kind, and he that knew himself, came at length to the Superstantial of every way substantial good.

40. But he that through the Error of Love, loved the Body, abideth wandering in darkness, sensible, suffering the things of death.

41. Trismegistus:—But why do they that are ignorant, sin so much, that they should therefore be deprived of immortality?

42. Pimander:—Thou seemest not to have understood what thou hast heard.

43. Trismegistus:—Peradventure I seem so to thee, but I both understand and remember them.

44. Pimander:—I am glad for thy sake, if thou understoodest them.

45. Trismegistus:—Tell me, why are they worthy of death, that are in death?

46. PIMANDER:—Because there goeth a sad and dismal darkness before its Body; of which darkness is the moist Nature, of which moist Nature, the Body consisteth in the sensible World, from whence death is derived. Has thou understood this aright?

47. TRISMEGISTUS:—But why, or how doth he that understands himself, go or pass into God?

48. PIMANDER:—That which the Word of God said, say I: Because the Father of all things consists of Life and Light, whereof Man is made.

49. TRISMEGISTUS:—Thou sayest very well.

50. PIMANDER:—God and the Father is Light and Life, of which Man is made. If therefore thou learn and believe thyself to be of the Life and Light, thou shalt again pass into Life.

51. TRISMEGISTUS:—But yet tell me more, O my Mind, how I shall go into Life?

52. PIMANDER:—God saith, Let the Man, endued with a Mind, mark, consider, and know himself well.

53. TRISMEGISTUS:—Have not all Men a mind?

54. PIMANDER:—Take heed what thou sayest, for I the Mind come unto men that are holy and good, pure and merciful, and that live piously and religiously; and my presence is a help unto them. And forthwith they know all things, and lovingly they supplicate and propitiate the Father; and blessing him, they give him thanks, and sing hymns unto him, being ordered and directed by filial Affection and natural Love: And before they give up their Bodies to the death of them, they hate their Senses, knowing their Works and Operations.

55. Rather I that am the Mind itself, will not suffer the Operations or Works, which happen or belong to the body, to be finished and brought to perfection in them; but being the Porter or Doorkeeper, I will shut up the entrances of Evil, and cut off the thoughtful desires of filthy works.

56. But to the foolish, and evil, and wicked, and envious, and covetous, and murderous, and profane, I am far off, giving place to the avenging Demon, which applying unto him the sharpness of fire, tormenteth such a man sensible, and armeth him the more to all wickedness, that he may obtain the greater punishment.

57. And such a one never ceaseth, having unfulfillable desires, and unsatisfiable concupiscences, and always fighting in darkness; for the Demon afflicts and tormenteth him continually, and increaseth the fire upon him more and more.

58. Trismegistus:—Thou hast, O Mind, most excellently taught me all things, as I desired; but tell me, moreover, after the return is made, what then?

59. Pimander:—First of all, in the resolution of the material Body, the Body itself is given up to alteration, and the form which it had, becometh invisible; and the idle manners are permitted, and left to the Demon, and the Senses of the Body return into their Fountains, being parts, and again made up into Operations.

60. And Anger, and Concupiscence go into the brutish or unreasonable Nature; and the rest striveth upward by Harmony.

61. And to the first Zone it giveth the power it had of increasing and diminishing.

62. To the second, the machinations or plotting of evils, and one effectual deceit or craft.

63. To the third, the idle deceit of Concupiscence.

64. To the fourth, the desire of Rule, and unsatiable Ambition.

65. To the fifth, profane Boldness, and headlong rashness of Confidence.

66. To the sixth, Evil and ineffectual occasions of Riches.

67. To the seventh Zone, subtle Falsehood, always lying in wait.

68. And then being made naked of all the Operations of Harmony, it cometh to the eighth Nature, having its proper power, and singeth praises to the Father with the things that are, and all they that are present rejoice, and congratulate the coming of it; and being made like to them with whom it converseth, it heareth also the Powers that are above the eighth Nature, singing praise to God in a certain voice that is peculiar to them.

69. And then in order they return unto the Father, and themselves deliver themselves to the Powers, and becoming Powers they are in God.

70. This is the Good, and to them that know, to be deified.[1]

71. Furthermore, why sayest thou, What resteth, but that understanding all men, thou become a guide, and way-leader to them that are worthy; that the kind of Humanity, or Mankind, may be saved by God?

72. When Pimander had thus said unto me, he was mingled among the Powers.

73. But I, giving thanks, and blessing the Father of all things, rose up, being enabled by him, and taught the Nature, of the Nature of the whole, and having seen the greatest sight or spectacle.

74. And I began to Preach unto men, the beauty and fairness of Piety and Knowledge.

75. O ye People, Men, born and made of the Earth, which have given Yourselves over to Drunkenness and Sleep, and to the Ignorance of God, be Sober and Cease your Surfeit, whereunto you are allured and visited by Brutish and Unreasonable Sleep.

76. And they that heard me, come willingly, and with one accord; and then I said further.

77. Why, O Men of the Offspring of the Earth, why have you delivered Yourselves over unto Death, having Power to Partake of Immortality? Repent and Change your Minds, you

that have together Walked in Error, and have been Darkened in Ignorance.

78. Depart from that dark Light, be Partakers of Immortality, and Leave or Forsake Corruption.

79. And some of Them That Heard Me, mocking and scorning, went away, and delivered themselves up to the way of Death.

80. But others, casting themselves down before my feet, besought me that they might be taught; but I, causing them to rise up, became a guide of mankind, teaching them the reasons how, and by what means they may be saved. And I sowed in them the words of Wisdom, and nourished them with Ambrosian Water of Immortality.

81. And when it was Evening, and the Brightness of the same began wholly to go down, {I commanded them to go down,}² I commanded them to give thanks to God; and when they had finished their thanksgiving, everyone returned to his own lodging.

82. But I wrote in myself the bounty and benevolence of Pimander; and being filled with what I most desired, I was exceedingly glad.

83. For the sleep of the Body was the sober watchfulness of the mind; and the shutting of my eyes the true Sight, and my silence great with child and full of good; and the pronouncing of my words, the blossoms and fruits of good things.

84. And thus it came to pass or happened unto me, which I received from my mind, that is, Pimander, the Lord of the Word; whereby I became inspired by God with the Truth.

85. For which cause, with my Soul, and whole strength, I give praise and blessing unto God the Father.

86. Holy is God, the Father of All Things.

87. Holy is God, Whose Will is Performed and Accomplished by His Own Powers.

88. Holy is God, that Determineth to be Known, and is Known by His Own, or Those that are His.

89. Holy art Thou, that by Thy Word has established all Things.

90. Holy art Thou, of Whom all Nature is the Image.

91. Holy art Thou, Whom Nature hath not Formed.

92. Holy art Thou, that art Stronger than all Power.

93. Holy art Thou, that art Greater[3] than all Excellency.

94. Holy art Thou, Who art Better than all Praise.

95. Accept these Reasonable Sacrifices from a Pure Soul, and a Heart stretched out unto Thee.

96. O Thou Unspeakable, Unutterable, to be Praised with Silence!

97. I beseech Thee, that I may never Err from the Knowledge of Thee, Look Mercifully upon Me, and Enable Me, and Enlighten with this Grace, those that are in Ignorance, the Brothers of my Kind, but thy Sons.

98. Therefore I Believe Thee, and Bear Witness, and go into the Life and Light.

99. Blessed art Thou, O Father, Thy Man would be Sanctified with Thee, as Thou hast given Him all Power.

THE END OF

## THE SECOND BOOK.

# THE THIRD BOOK,

CALLED

## "THE HOLY SERMON."

———

THE glory of all things, God, and that which is Divine, and the Divine Nature, the beginning of things that are.

2. God, and the Mind, and Nature, and Matter, and Operation, or Working, and Necessity, and the End, and Renovation.

3. For there were in the Chaos, an infinite darkness in the Abyss or bottomless Depth, and Water, and a subtle Spirit intelligible in Power; and there went out the Holy Light, and the Elements were coagulated from the Sand out of the moist Substance.

4. And all the Gods distinguished the Nature full of Seeds.

5. And when all things were interminated and unmade up, the light things were divided on high. And the heavy things were founded upon the moist sand, all things being Terminated or Divided by Fire; and being sustained or hung up by the Spirit, they were so carried, and the Heaven was seen in Seven Circles.

6. And the Gods were seen in their Ideas of the Stars, with all their Signs, and the Stars were numbered, with the Gods in them. And the Sphere was all lined with Air, carried about in a circular motion by the Spirit of God.

7. And every God, by his internal power, did that which was commanded him; and there were made four-footed things, and creeping things, and such as live in the Water, and such

as fly, and every fruitful Seed, and Grass, and the Flowers of all Greens, and which had sowed in themselves the Seeds of Regeneration.

8. As also the Generations of Men, to the Knowledge of the Divine Works, and a lively or working Testimony of Nature, and a multitude of Men, and the Dominion of all things under Heaven, and the Knowledge of good things, and to be increased in increasing, and multiplied in multitude.

9. And every Soul in flesh, by the wonderful working of the Gods in the Circles, to the beholding of Heaven, the Gods, Divine Works, and the Operations of Nature; and for Signs of good things, and the Knowledge of the Divine Power, and to find out every cunning workmanship of good things.

10. So it beginneth to live in them, and to be wise according to the Operation of the course of the circular Gods; and to be resolved into that which shall be great Monuments and Rememberances of the cunning Works done upon Earth, leaving them to be read by the darkness of times.

11. And every Generation of living Flesh, of Fruit, Seed, and all Handicrafts, though they be lost, must of necessity be renewed by the renovation of the Gods, and of the Nature of a Circle, moving in number; for it is a Divine thing that every world temperature should be renewed by Nature; for in that which is Divine, is Nature also established.[4]

THE END OF

THE FRAGMENTS OF

## THE THIRD BOOK.

*(Very Imperfect.)*

# THE FOURTH BOOK,

## "THE KEY."

———

YESTERDAY's Speech, O Asclepius, I dedicated to thee; this day it is fit to dedicate to Tat, because it is an Epitome of those general Speeches which were spoken to him.

2. God therefore, and the Father, and the Good, O Tat, have the same Nature, or rather also the same Act and Operation.

3. For there is one name or appellation of Nature or Increase, which concerneth things changeable, and another about things unchangeable, and about things unmoveable, that is to say, Things Divine and Humane; every one of which, himself will have so to be; but action or operation is of another thing, or elsewhere, as we have taught in other things, Divine and Humane, which must here also be understood.[5]

4. For his Operation or Act, is his Will, and his Essence, to Will all Things to be.

5. For what is God, and the Father, and the Good, but the Being of all things that yet are not, and the existence itself, of those things that are?

6. This is God, this is the Father, this is the Good, whereunto no other thing is present or approacheth.

7. For the World, and the Sun, which is also a Father by Participation, is not for all that equally the cause of Good, and of Life, to living Creatures: And if this be so, he is altogether constrained by the Will of the Good, without which it is not possible, either to be, or to be begotten or made.

8. But the Father is the cause of his Children, who hath a will both to sow and nourish that which is good by the Sun.[6]

9. For Good is always active or busy in making; and this cannot be in any other, but in him that taketh nothing, and yet willeth all things to be; for I will not say, O Tat, making them; for he that maketh is defective in much time, in which sometimes he maketh not, as also of quantity and quality; for sometimes he maketh those things that have quantity and quality, and sometimes the contrary.

10. But God is the Father, and the Good, in being all things; for he both will be this, and is it, and yet all this for himself (as is true) in him that can see it.

11. For all things else are for this, it is the property of Good to be known: This is the Good, O Tat.

12. Tat:—Thou hast filled us, O Father, with a sight both good and fair, and the eye of my mind is almost become more holy by the sight or spectacle.

13. Trismegistus:—I wonder not at It, for the Sight of Good is not like the Beam of the Sun, which being of a fiery shining brightness, maketh the eye blind by his excessive Light, that gazeth upon it; rather the contrary, for it enlighteneth, and so much increaseth the light of the eye, as any man is able to receive the influence of this intelligible clearness.

14. For it is more swift and sharp to pierce, and innocent or harmless withal, and full of immortality, and they are capable, and can draw any store of this spectacle and sight, do many times fall asleep from the Body, into this most fair and beauteous Vision; which thing Celius and Saturn our Progenitors obtained unto.

15. Tat:—I would we also, O Father, could do so.

16. Trismegistus:—I would we could, O Son; but for the present we are less intent to the Vision, and cannot yet open the eyes of our minds to behold the incorruptible, and

incomprehensible Beauty of that Good: But then we shall see it, when we have nothing at all to say of it.

17. For the knowledge of it, is a Divine Silence, and the rest of all the Senses; For neither can he that understands that understand anything else, nor he that sees that, see anything else, nor hear any other thing, nor in sum, move the Body.

18. For shining steadfastly upon, and round about the whole Mind it enlighteneth all the Soul; and loosing it from the Bodily Senses and Motions, it draweth it from the Body, and changeth it wholly into the Essence of God.

19. For it is Possible for the Soul, O Son, to be Deified while yet it Lodgeth in the Body of Man, if it Contemplate the Beauty of the Good.

20. TAT:—How dost thou mean deifying, Father?

21. TRISMEGISTUS:—There are differences, O Son, of every Soul.

22. TAT:—But how dost thou again divide the changes?

23. TRISMEGISTUS:—Hast thou not heard in the general Speeches, that from one Soul of the Universe, are all those Souls, which in all the world are tossed up and down, as it were, and severally divided? Of these Souls there are many changes, some into a more fortunate estate, and some quite the contrary; for they which are of creeping things, are changed into those of watery things; and those of things living in the water, to those of things living upon the Land; and Airy ones are changed into men, and human Souls, that lay hold of immortality, are changed into Demons.

24. And so they go on into the Sphere or Region of the fixed Gods, for there are two choirs or companies of Gods, one of them that wander, and another of them that are fixed. And this is the perfect glory of the Soul.

25. But the Soul entering into the Body of a Man, if it continues Evil, shall neither taste of immortality, nor is partaker of the Good.

26. But being drawn back the same way, it returneth into creeping things. And this is the condemnation of an Evil Soul.

27. And the wickedness of a Soul is ignorance; for the Soul that knows nothing of the things that are, neither the Nature of them, nor that which is good, but is blinded, rusheth and dasheth against the bodily Passions, and unhappy as it is, and not knowing itself, it serveth strange Bodies, and evil ones, carrying the Body as a burden, and not ruling, but ruled. And this is the mischief of the Soul.

28. On the contrary, the virtue of the Soul is Knowledge; for he that knows is both good and religious, and already Divine.

29. Tat:—But who is such a one, O Father?

30. Trismegistus:—He that neither speaks, nor hears many things; for he, O Son, that heareth two speeches, or hearings, fighteth in the shadow.

31. For God, and the Father, and Good, is neither spoken nor heard.

32. This being so in all things that are, are the Senses, because they cannot be without them.

33. But Knowledge differs much from Sense; for Sense is of things that surmount it, but Knowledge is the end of Sense.

34. Knowledge is the gift of God; for all Knowledge is unbodily, but useth the Mind as an Instrument, as the Mind useth the Body.

35. Therefore, both intelligible and material things, go both of them into bodies; for, of contraposition, That is, Setting One against Another, and Contrariety, all Things must Consist. And it is impossible it should be otherwise.

36. Tat:—Who, therefore, is this Material God?

37. Trismegistus:—The fair and beautiful World, and yet it is not good; for it is material, and easily passible, nay, it is the first of all passible things; and the second of the things that are, and needy or wanting somewhat else. And it was once made, and

is always, and is ever in generation, and made, and continually makes, or generates things that have quantity and quality.

38. For it is moveable, and every material motion is generation; but the intellectual stability moves the material motion after this manner.

39. Because the World is a Sphere, that is a Head, and above the head there is nothing material, as beneath the feet there is nothing intellectual.

40. The whole Universe is material; The Mind is the head, and it is moved spherically, that is like a head.

41. Whatsoever, therefore, is joined or united to the Membrane or Film of this head, wherein the Soul is, is immortal, and as in the Soul of a made Body, hath its Soul full of the Body; but those that are further from that Membrane, have the Body full of Soul.

42. The whole is a living wight, and therefore consisteth of material and intellectual.

43. And the World is the first, and Man the second living wight after the World; but the first of things that are mortal; and therefore hath whatsoever benefit of the Soul all the other have: And yet for all this, he is not only not good, but flatly evil, as being mortal.

44. For the World is not good, as it is moveable; nor evil as it is immortal.

45. But man is evil, both as he is moveable, and as he is mortal.

46. But the Soul of Man is carried in this manner, The Mind is in Reason, Reason in the Soul, The Soul in the Spirit, The Spirit in the Body.

47. The Spirit being diffused and going through the veins, and arteries, and blood, both moveth the living Creature, and after a certain manner beareth it.

48. Wherefore some also have thought the Soul to be blood, being deceived in Nature, not knowing that first the Spirit must

return into the Soul, and then the blood is congealed, and the veins and arteries emptied, and then the living thing dieth: And this is the death of the Body.

49. All things depend of one beginning, and the beginning depends of that which is one and alone.

50. And the beginning is moved, that it may again be a beginning; but that which is one, standeth and abideth, and is not moved.

51. There are therefore, these three, God the Father, and the Good, the World, and Man: God hath the World, and the World hath Man; and the World is the Son of God, and Man as it were the Offspring of the World.

52. For God is not ignorant of Man, but knows him perfectly, and will be known by him. This only is healthful to man; the Knowledge of God: this is the return of Olympus; by this only the Soul is made good, and not sometimes good, and sometimes evil, but of necessity Good.

53. TAT:—What meaneth thou, O Father?

54. TRISMEGISTUS:—Consider, O Son, the Soul of a Child, when as yet it hath as yet received no dissolution of its Body, which is not yet grown, but is very small; how then if it look upon itself, it sees itself beautiful, as not having been as yet spotted with the Passions of the Body, but as it were depending yet upon the Soul of the World.

55. But when the Body is grown, and distracteth, the Soul it engenders Forgetfulness, and partakes no more of the Fair and the Good, and Forgetfulness is Evilness.

56. The like also happeneth to them that go out of the Body: for when the Soul runs back into itself, the Spirit is contracted into the blood, and the Soul into the Spirit; but the Mind being made pure, and free from these clothings; and being Divine by Nature, taking a fiery Body rangeth abroad in every place, leaving the Soul to judgment, and to the punishment it hath deserved.

57. Tat:—Why dost thou say so, O Father, that the Mind is separated from the Soul, and the Soul from the Spirit? When even now thou saidst that the Soul was the Clothing or Apparel of the Mind, and the Body of the Soul.

58. Trismegistus:—O Son, he that hears must co-understand, and conspire in thought with him that speaks; yea, he must have his hearing swifter and sharper than the voice of the speaker.

59. The disposition of these Clothings or Covers, is done in an Earthly Body; for it is impossible, that the Mind should establish or rest itself, naked, and of itself; in an Earthly Body; neither is the Earthly Body able to bear such immortality; and therefore, that it might suffer so great virtue, the Mind compacted, as it were, and took to itself the passible Body of the Soul, as a Covering or Clothing. And the Soul being also in some sort Divine, useth the Spirit as her Minister or Servant, and the Spirit governeth the living thing.

60. When therefore the Mind is separated, and departeth from the Earthly Body, presently it puts on its Fiery Coat, which it could not do, having to dwell in an Earthly Body.

61. For the Earth cannot suffer fire, for it is all burned of a small spark; therefore is the water poured round about the Earth, as a Wall or defence, to withstand the flame of fire.

62. But the Mind being the most sharp or swift of all the Divine Cogitations, and more swift than all the Elements, hath the fire for its Body.

63. For the Mind, which is the Workman of all, useth the fire as his instrument in his Workmanship; and he that is the Workman of all, useth it to the making of all things, as it is used by Man, to the making of Earthly things only; for the Mind that is upon Earth, void, or naked of fire, cannot do the business of men, nor that which is otherwise the affairs of God.

64. But the Soul of Man, and yet not everyone, but that which is pious and religious, is Angelical and Divine. And such

a Soul, after it is departed from the Body, having striven the strife of Piety, becomes either Mind or God.

65. And the strife of Piety is to know God, and to injure no Man, and this way it becomes Mind.

66. But the impious Soul abideth in its own essence, punished of itself, and seeking an earthly and humane Body to enter into.

67. For no other Body is capable of a Human Soul, neither is it lawful for a Man's Soul to fall into the Body of an unreasonable living thing: for it is the Law or Decree of God, to preserve a Human Soul from so great a contumely and reproach.

68. TAT:—How then is the Soul of Man punished, O Father, and what is its greatest torment?

69. HERMES:—Impiety, O my Son; for what Fire hath so great a flame as it? Or what biting Beast doth so tear the Body as it doth the Soul?

70. Or dost thou not see how many Evils the wicked Soul suffereth, roaring and crying out, I am Burned, I am Consumed, I know not what to Say or Do, I am Devoured, Unhappy Wretch, of the Evils that compass and lay hold upon me; Miserable that I am, I neither See nor Hear anything.

71. These are the voices of a punished and tormented Soul, and not as many; and thou, O Son, thinkest that the Soul going out of the Body grows brutish or enters into a Beast: which is a very great Error, for the Soul punished after this manner.

72. For the Mind, when it is ordered or appointed to get a fiery Body for the services of God, coming down into the wicked Soul, torments it with the whips of Sins, wherewith the wicked Soul, being scourged, turns itself to Murders and Contumelies, and Blasphemies, and divers Violences, and other things by which men are injured.

73. But into a pious Soul, the Mind entering, leads it into the Light of Knowledge.

74. And such a Soul is never satisfied with singing praise to God, and speaking well of all men; and both in words and deeds, always doing good in imitation of her Father.

75. Therefore, O Son, we must give thanks, and pray, that we may obtain a good mind.

76. The Soul therefore may be altered or changed into the better, but into the worse it is impossible.

77. But there is a communion of Souls, and those of Gods, communicate with those men; and those of men, with those of Beasts.

78. And the better always take of the worse, Gods of Men, Men of brute Beasts, but God of all: For He is the best of all, and all things are less than He.

79. Therefore is the World subject unto God, Man unto the World, and unreasonable things to Man.

80. But God is above all, and about all; and the beams of God are operations; and the beams of the World are Natures; and the beams of Man are Arts and Sciences.

81. And Operations do act by the World, and upon Man by the natural beams of the World, but Natures work by the Elements, and Man by Arts and Sciences.

82. And this is the Government of the whole, depending upon the Nature of the One, and piercing or coming down by the One Mind, than which nothing is more Divine, and more efficacious or operative; and nothing more uniting, or nothing is more One. The Communion of Gods to Men, and of Men to Gods.

83. This is the Bonus Genius, or good Demon, blessed Soul that is fullest of it! And unhappy Soul that is empty of it!

84. TAT:—And wherefore, Father?

85. TRISMEGISTUS:—Know, Son, that every Soul hath the Good Mind; for of that it is we now speak, and not of that Minister of whom we said before, That he was sent from the Judgment.

86. For the Soul without the Mind, can neither do, nor say anything; for many times the Mind flies away from the Soul, and in that hour the Soul neither seeth nor heareth, but is like an unreasonable thing; so great is the power of the Mind.

87. But neither brooketh it an idle or lazy Soul, but leaves such a one fastened to the Body, and by it is pressed down.

88. And such a Soul, O Son, hath no Mind; wherefore neither must such a one be called a Man.

89. For Man is a Divine living thing, and is not to be compared to any brute Beast that lives upon Earth, but to them that are above in Heaven, that are called Gods.

90. Rather, if we shall be bold to speak the truth, he that is a Man indeed, is above them, or at least they are equal in power, one to the other. For none of the things in Heaven will come down upon Earth, and leave the limits of Heaven, but a Man ascends up into Heaven, and measures it.

91. And he knoweth what things are on high, and what below, and learneth all other things exactly.

92. And that which is the greatest of all, he leaveth not the Earth, and yet is above: So great is the greatness of his Nature.

93. Wherefore we must be bold to say, That an Earthly Man is a mortal God, and That the Heavenly God is an Immortal Man.

94. Wherefore, by these two are all things governed, the World and Man; but they and all things else, of that which is One.

THE END OF

THE FOURTH BOOK.

# THE FIFTH BOOK,

## "THAT GOD IS NOT MANIFEST,

## AND YET MOST MANIFEST."

―――

THIS Discourse, I will also make to thee, O Tat, that thou mayest not be ignorant of the more excellent Name of God.

2. But do thou contemplate in thy Mind, how that which to many seems hidden, and unmanifest, may be most manifest to thee.

3. For it were not all, if it were apparent, for whatsoever is apparent, is generated or made; for it was made manifest, but that which is not manifest is ever.

4. For it needeth not be manifested, for it is always.

5. And he maketh all other things manifest, being unmanifest, as being always, and making other things manifest, he is not made manifest.

6. Himself is not made, yet in fantasy he fantasieth all things, or in appearance he maketh them appear, for appearance is only of those things that are generated or made, for appearance is nothing but generation.

7. But he is that One, that is not made nor generated, is also unapparent and unmanifest.

8. But making all things appear, he appeareth in all, and by all; but especially he is manifested to, or in those things wherein himself listeth.

9. Thou, therefore, O Tat, my Son, pray first to the Lord and Father, and to the Alone, and to the One, from whom is one

to be merciful to thee, that thou mayest know and understand so great a God; and that he would shine one of his beams upon thee in thy understanding.

10. For only the Understanding sees that which is not manifest, or apparent, as being itself not manifest or apparent; and if thou canst, O Tat, it will appear to the eyes of thy Mind.

11. For the Lord, void of envy, appeareth through the whole world. Thou mayest see the intelligence, and take it into thy hands, and contemplate the Image of God.

12. But if that which is in thee, be not known or apparent unto thee, how shall he in thee be seen, and appear unto thee by the eyes?

13. But if thou wilt see him, consider and understand the Sun, consider the course of the Moon, consider the order of the Stars.

14. Who is he that keepeth order? For all order is circumscribed or terminated in number and place.

15. The Sun is the greatest of the Gods in Heaven, to whom all the Heavenly Gods give place, as to a King and Potentate; and yet he being such a one, greater than the Earth or the Sea, is content to suffer infinite lesser stars to walk and move above himself; whom doth he fear the while, O Son?

16. Every one of these Stars that are in Heaven, do not make the like, or an equal course; who is it that hath prescribed unto every one, the manner and the greatness of their course?

17. This Bear that turns round about its own self; and carries round the whole World with her, who possessed and made such an Instrument?

18. Who hath set the Bounds to the Sea? Who hath established the Earth? For there is somebody, O Tat, that is the Maker and Lord of these things.

19. For it is impossible, O Son, that either place, or number, or measure, should be observed without a Maker.

20. For no order can be made by disorder or disproportion.

21. I would it were possible for thee, O my Son, to have wings, and to fly into the Air, and being taken up in the midst, between Heaven and Earth, to see the stability of the Earth, the fluidness of the Sea, the courses of the Rivers, the largeness of the Air, the sharpness and swiftness of the Fire, the motion of the Stars; and the speediness of the Heaven, by which it goeth round about all these.

22. O Son, what a happy sight it were, at one instant, to see all these, that which is immoveable moved, and that which is hidden appear and be manifest.

23. And if thou wilt see and behold this Workman, even by mortal things that are upon Earth, and in the deep, consider, O Son, how Man is made and framed in the Womb; and examine diligently the skill and cunning of the Workman, and learn who it was that wrought and fashioned the beautiful and Divine shape of Man; who circumscribed and marked out his eyes? Who bored his nostrils and ears? Who opened his mouth? Who stretched out and tied together his sinews? Who channelled the veins? Who hardened and made strong the bones? Who clothed the flesh with skin? Who divided the fingers and joints? Who flatted and made broad the soles of the feet? Who digged the pores? Who stretched out the spleen? Who made the heart like a Pyramis? Who made the Liver broad? Who made the Lights spungy, and full of holes? Who made the belly large and capacious? Who set to outward view the more honourable parts, and hid the filthy ones?

24. See how many Arts in one Matter, and how many Works in one Superscription, and all exceedingly beautiful, and all done in measure, and yet all differing.

25. Who hath made all these things? What Mother? What Father? Save only God that is not manifest; that made all things by his own Will.

26. And no man says that a statue or an image is made without a Carver or a Painter, and was this Workmanship made

without a Workman? O great Blindness! O great Impiety! O great Ignorance!

27. Never, O Son Tat, canst thou deprive the Workmanship of the Workman, rather, it is the best Name of all the Names of God, to call him the Father of all, for so he is alone; and this is his work to be the Father.

28. And if thou wilt force me to say anything more boldly, it is his Essence to be pregnant, or great with all things, and to make them.

29. And as without a Maker, it is impossible that anything should be made, so it is that he should not always be, and always be making all things in Heaven, in the Air, in the Earth, in the Deep, in the whole World, and in every part of the whole that is, or that is not.

30. For there is nothing in the whole World, that is not himself, both the things that are, and the things that are not.

31. For the things that are, he hath made manifest; and the things that are not, he hath hid in himself.

32. This is God that is better than any name; this is he that is secret; this is he that is most manifest; this is he that is to be seen by the Mind; this is he that is visible to the Eye; this is he that hath no Body; and this is he that hath many Bodies; rather, there is nothing of any body, which is not He.

33. For he alone is all things.

34. And for this cause He hath all Names, because He is the One Father; and therefore He hath no Name, because He is the Father of all.

35. Who therefore can bless thee, or give thanks for thee, or to thee?

36. Which way shall I look, when I praise thee? Upward? Downward? Outward? Inward?

37. For about thee there is no manner, nor place, nor anything else of all things that are.

38. But all things are in thee; all things from thee, thou givest all things, and takest nothing; for thou hast all things; and there is nothing that thou hast not.

39. When shall I praise thee, O Father; for it is neither possible to comprehend thy hour, nor thy time?

40. For what shall I praise thee? For what thou hast made, or for what thou hast not made? For those things thou hast manifested, or for those things thou hast hidden?

41. Wherefore shall I praise thee as being of myself, or having anything of mine own, or rather being another's?

42. For thou art what I am, thou art what I do, thou art what I say.

43. Thou Art All Things, and there is Nothing Else Thou Art Not.

44. Thou Art Thou, All that is Made, and All that is not Made.

45. The Mind that Understandeth.

46. The Father that Maketh and Frameth.

47. The Good that Worketh.

48. The Good that doth All Things.

49. Of the Matter, the most subtle and slender is Air, of the Air the Soul, of the Soul the Mind, of the Mind God.

THE END OF

## THE FIFTH BOOK.

# THE SIXTH BOOK,

## "THAT IN GOD ALONE IS GOOD."

———

Good, O Asclepius, is in nothing but in God alone; or rather God himself is the Good always.

2. And if it be so, then must he be an Essence or Substance, void of all Motion and Generation; but nothing is void or empty of him.

3. And this Essence hath about or in himself a Stable and firm Operation, wanting nothing, most full, and giving abundantly.

4. One thing is the Beginning of all things, for it giveth all things; and when I name the Good, I mean that which is altogether and always Good.

5. This is present to none, but God alone; for he wanteth nothing, that he should desire to have it, nor can anything be taken from him; the loss whereof may grieve him; for sorrow is a part of evilness.

6. Nothing is stronger than he, that he should be opposed by it; nor nothing equal to him, that he should be in love with it; nothing unheard of to be angry, with nothing wiser to be envious at.

7. And none of these being in his Essence, what remains, but only the Good?

8. For as in this, being such an Essence, there is none of the evils; so in none of the other things shall the Good be found.

9. For in all other things, are all those other things, as well in the small as the great; and as well in the particulars as in this living Creature, the greater and mightiest of all.

10. For all things that are made or generated, are full of Passion, Generation itself being a Passion; and where Passion is, there is not the Good; where the Good is, there is no Passion; where it is day, it is not night; where it is night, it is not day.

11. Wherefore it is impossible, that in Generation should be the Good, but only in that which is not generated or made.

12. Yet as the Participation of all things is in the Matter bound, so also of that which is Good. After this manner is the World Good, as it maketh all things, and in the part of making or doing it is Good, but in all other things not good.

13. For it is passable, and moveable, and the Maker of passable things.

14. In Man also the Good is ordered (or Taketh Denomination) in comparison of that which is evil; for that which is not very Evil, is here Good; and that which is here called Good, is the least particle, or proportion of Evil.

15. It is impossible therefore, that the Good should be here pure from Evil; for here the Good groweth Evil, and growing Evil, it doth not still abide Good; and not abiding Good, it becomes Evil.

16. Therefore in God alone is the Good, or rather God is the Good.

17. Therefore, O Asclepius, there is nothing in men (or among Men) but the name of Good, the thing itself is not, for it is impossible; for a material Body receiveth (or Comprehendeth), is not as being on every side encompassed and coacted with evilness, and labours, and griefs, and desires, and wrath, and deceits, and foolish opinions.

18. And in that which is the worst of all, Asclepius, every one of the forenamed things, is here believed to be the greatest Good, especially that supreme mischief the pleasures of the

Belly, and the ring-leader of all evils. Error is here the absence of the Good.

19. And I give thanks unto God, that, concerning the knowledge of Good, put this assurance in my Mind, that it is impossible it should be in the World.

20. For the World is the fulness of evilness; but God is the fulness of Good, or Good of God.

21. For the eminencies of all appearing Beauty, are in the Essence more pure, and more sincere, and peradventure they are also the Essences of it.

22. For we must be bold to say, Asclepius, that the Essence of God, if he have an Essence, is that which is fair or beautiful; but no good is comprehended in this World.

23. For all things that are subject to the eye, are Idols, and as it were Shadows; but those things that are not subject to the eye, are ever, especially the Essence of the Fair, and the Good.

24. And as the eye cannot see God, so neither the Fair, and the Good.

25. For these are the parts of God that partake the Nature of the whole, proper, and familiar unto him alone, inseparable, most lovely, whereof either God is enamoured, or they are enamoured of God.

26. If thou canst understand God, thou shall understand the Fair, and the Good, which is most shining, and enlightening, and most enlightened by God.

27. For that Beauty is above comparison, and that Good is inimitable, as God himself.

28. As, therefore, thou understandest God, so understand the Fair and the Good; for these are incommunicable to any other living creatures, because they are inseparable from God.

29. If thou seek concerning God, thou seekest or askest also of the Fair, for there is one way that leads to the same thing, that is Piety with Knowledge.

30. Wherefore, they that are ignorant, and go not in the way of Piety, dare call Men Fair and Good, never seeing so much as in a dream, what good is; but being enfolded and wrapped upon all evil, and believing that the Evil is the Good, they, by that means, both use it unsatiably, and are afraid to be deprived of it; and therefore they strive, by all possible means, that they may not only have it, but also increase it.

31. Such, O Asclepius, are the Good, and Fair things of Men, which we can neither love nor hate; for this is the hardest thing of all, that we have need of them, and cannot live without them.

THE END OF

## THE SIXTH BOOK.

# THE SEVENTH BOOK,

## "HIS SECRET SERMON IN THE MOUNT

## OF REGENERATION, AND

## THE PROFESSION OF SILENCE."

———

### To His Son Tat.

Tat:—In the general Speeches, O Father, discoursing of the Divinity, thou speakest enigmatically, and didst not clearly reveal thyself, saying, That no man can be saved before Regeneration.

2. And when I did humbly entreat thee, at the going up to the Mountain, after thou hadst discoursed unto me, having a great desire, to learn this Argument of Regeneration; because among all the rest, I am ignorant only of this thou toldst me thou wouldst impart it to me, when I would estrange myself from the world: whereupon I made myself ready, and have vindicated the understanding that is in me, from the deceit of the World.

3. Now, then fulfil my defect, and as thou saidst, instruct me of Regeneration, either by word of mouth or secretly; for I know not, O Trismegistus, of what Substance, or what Womb or what Seed a Man is thus born.

4. Hermes:—O Son, this Wisdom is to be understood in silence, and the Seed is the true Good.

5. Tat:—Who soweth it, O Father? For I am utterly ignorant and doubtful.

6. HERMES:—The Will of God, O Son.

7. And what manner of Man is he that is thus born? For in this point, I am clean deprived of the Essence that understandeth in me.

8. HERMES:—The Son of God will be another. God made the universe, that in everything consisteth of all powers.

9. TAT:—Thou tellest me a Riddle, Father, and dost not speak as a Father to a Son.

10. HERMES:—Son, things of this kind are not taught, but are by God, when he pleaseth, brought to remembrance.

11. TAT:—Thou speakest of things strained, or far-fetched, and impossible, Father; and therefore I will directly contradict them.

12. HERMES:—Wilt thou prove a Stranger, Son, to thy Father's kind?

13. TAT:—Do not envy me, Father, or pardon me, I am thy Natural Son; discourse unto me the manner of Regeneration.

14. HERMES:—What shall I say, O my Son? I have nothing to say more than this, that I see in myself an unfeigned sight[7] or spectacle, made by the mercy of God, and I am gone out of myself into an immortal body, and am not now, what I was before, but was begotten in Mind.

15. This thing is not taught, nor is it to be seen in this formed Element; for which the first compounded form was neglected by me; and that I am now separated from it; for I have both the touch and the measure of it, yet am I now estranged from them.

16. Thou seest, O Son, with thine eyes; but though thou never look so steadfastly upon me, with the Body, and the bodily sight, thou canst not see, nor understand what I am now.

17. TAT:—Thou hast driven me, O Father, into no small fury and distraction of mind, for I do not now see myself.

18. HERMES:—I would, O Son, that thou also wert gone out of thyself, like them that Dream in their sleep.

19. TAT:—Then tell me this, who is the Author and Maker of Regeneration?

20. HERMES:—The Child of God, one Man by the Will of God.

21. TAT:—Now, O Father, thou hast put me to silence for ever, and all my former thoughts have quite left and forsaken me, for I see the greatness, and shape of things here below, and nothing but falsehood in them all.

22. And so thence this mortal Form is daily changed, and turned by time into increase, and diminution, as being falsehood; what therefore is true, O Trismegistus?

23. TRISMEGISTUS:—That, O my Son, which is not troubled, nor bounded; not coloured, not figured, not changed; that which is naked, bright,[8] comprehensible only of itself, unalterable, unbodily.

24. TAT:—Now I am mad, indeed, O Father; for when I thought me to have been made a wise man by thee, with these thoughts, thou hast quite dulled all my senses.

25. HERMES:—Yet is it so, as I say, O Son, He that Looketh Only upon that which is carried upward as Fire, that which is carried downward as Earth, that which is moist as Water, and that which bloweth, or is subject to blast, as Air; how can he sensibly understand that which is neither hard, nor moist, nor tangible, nor perspicuous, seeing it is only understood in power and operation? But I beseech and pray to the Mind, which alone can understand the Generation which is in God.

26. TAT:—Then am I, O Father, utterly unable to do it.

27. HERMES:—God forbid, Son, rather draw or pull him unto thee (or Study to Know Him) and he will come, be but Willing, and it shall be done; quite (or make idle) the Senses of the Body, purging thyself from the unreasonable brutish torments of matter.

28. TAT:—Have I any (revengers or) tormentors in myself, Father?

29. HERMES:—Yes, and those, not a few, but many, and fearful ones.

30. TAT:—I do not know them, Father.

31. HERMES:—One Torment, Son, is Ignorance: a second, Sorrow; a third, Intemperance; a fourth, Concupiscence; a fifth, Injustice; a sixth, Covetousness; a seventh, Deceit; an eighth, Envy; a ninth, Fraud or Guile; a tenth, Wrath; an eleventh, Rashness; a twelfth, Maliciousness.

32. They are in number twelve, and under these many more; some which through the prison of the Body, do force the inwardly placed Man to suffer sensibly.

33. And they do not suddenly, or easily depart from him, that hath obtained mercy of God; and herein consists, both the manner and the reason of Regeneration.

34. For the rest, O Son, hold thy peace, and praise God in silence, and by that means, the mercy of God will not cease, or be wanting unto us.

35. Therefore, rejoice, my Son, from henceforward, being purged by the powers of God, to the Knowledge of the Truth.

36. For the revelation of God is come to us, and when that came, all Ignorance was cast out.

37. The Knowledge of Joy is come unto us, and when that comes, Sorrow shall fly away to them that are capable of it.

38. I call unto Joy, the power of Temperance, a power whose Virtue is most sweet; Let us take her unto ourselves, O Son, most willingly, for how at her coming hath she put away Intemperance?

39. Now I call the forth, Continence, the power which is over Concupiscence. This, O Son, is the stable and firm foundation of Justice.

40. For see, how without labour, she hath chased away Injustice, and we are justified, O Son, when Injustice is away.

41. The sixth Virtue, which comes into us, I call Communion, which is against Covetousness.

42. And when that (Covetousness) is gone, I call Truth, and when she cometh, Error and Deceit vanisheth.

43. See, O Son, how the Good is fulfilled by the access of Truth; for by this means Envy is gone from us; for Truth is accompanied with the Good, together also with Life and Light.

44. And there came no more any torment of Darkness, but being overcome, they all fled away suddenly and tumultuously.

45. Thou hast understood, O Son, the manner of Regeneration; for upon the coming of these Ten, the Intellectual Generation is perfected, and then it driveth away the Twelve; and we have seen it in the Generation itself.

46. Whosoever therefore hath of Mercy obtained this Generation, which is according to God, he leaving all bodily sense, knoweth himself to consist of divine things, and rejoiceth, being made by God stable and immutable.

47. TAT:—O Father, I conceive and understand, not by the sight of mine eyes, but by the Intellectual Operation, which is by the Powers. I am in Heaven, in the Earth, in the Water, in the Air, I am in Living Creatures, in Plants, in the Womb, everywhere.

48. Yet tell me, further, this one thing, How are the Torments of Darkness, being in number Twelve, driven away and expelled by the Ten Powers? What is the manner of it, Trismegistus?

49. HERMES:—This Tabernacle, O Son, consists of the Zodiacal Circle; and this consisting of Twelve numbers, the Idea of one; but all formed Nature admit divers Conjugations to the deceiving of Man.

50. And though they be different in themselves, yet are they united in practice (as, for example, Rashness is inseparable from Anger), and they are also indeterminate: Therefore, with good Reason do they make their departure, being driven away by the Ten Powers; that is to say, By the dead.

51. For the number of Ten, O Son, is the Begetter of Souls. And there Life and Light are united, where the number of Unity is born of the Spirit.

52. Therefore, according to Reason, Unity hath the number of Ten, and the number of Ten hath Unity.

53. TAT:—O Father, I now see the Universe, and myself in the Mind.

54. HERMES:—This is Regeneration, O Son, that we should not any longer fix our imagination upon this Body, subject to the three dimensions, according to this, according to this Speech which we have now commented. That we may not at all caluminate the Universe.

55. TAT:—Tell me, O Father, This Body that consists of Powers, shall it ever admit of Dissolution?

56. HERMES:—Good words, Son, and speak not things impossible; for so thou shalt sin, and the eye of thy mind grow wicked.

57. The sensible Body of Nature is far from the Essential Generation; for that is subject to Dissolution, but this is not; and that is mortal, but this immortal. Dost thou not know that thou art born a God, and the Son of the One, as I am?

58. TAT:—How feign would I, O Father, hear that praise given by a Hymn, which thou sadist, thou heardest from the Powers, when I was in the Octonary?

59. HERMES:—As Pimander said, by way of Oracle to the Octonary, Thou dost well, O Son, to desire the Solution of the Tabernacle, for thou art purified.

60. Pimander, the Mind of Absolute Power and Authority, hath delivered no more unto me, than those that are written; knowing that of myself, I can understand all things, and hear, and see what I will. And he commanded me to do those things that are good; and therefore all the Powers that are in me sing.

61. TAT:—I would hear thee, O Father, and understand these things.

62. HERMES:—Be quiet, O Son, and now hearken to that harmonious blessing and thanksgiving: the hymn of Regeneration, which I did not determine to have spoken of so plainly, but to thyself in the end of all.

63. Wherefore, this is not taught, but hid in silence.

64. So then, O Son, do thou, standing in the open Air, worship, looking to the North Wind, about the going down of the Sun; and to the South, when the Sun ariseth; And now keep silence, Son.

## THE SECRET SONG.
### THE HOLY SPEECH.

65. LET all the Nature of the World entertain the hearing of this Hymn.

66. Be opened, O Earth, and let all the Treasure of the Rain be opened.

67. You Trees, tremble not, for I will sing and praise the Lord of the Creation, and the All, and the One.

68. Be opened, you Heavens, ye Winds stand still, and let the Immortal Circle of God receive these words.

69. For I will sing, and praise him that created all things, that fixed the Earth, and hung up the Heavens, and commanded the sweet Water to come out of the Ocean; into all the World inhabited, and not inhabited, to the use and nourishment of all things, or men.

70. That commanded the fire to shine for every action, both to Gods and Men.

71. Let us altogether give him blessing, which rideth upon the Heavens, the Creator of all Nature.

72. This is he that is the Eye of the Mind, and Will accept the praise of my Powers.

73. O all ye Powers that are in me, praise the One, and All.

74. Sing together with my Will, all you Powers that are in me.

75. O Holy Knowledge, being enlightened by thee, I magnify the intelligible Light, and rejoice in the Joy of the Mind.

76. All my Powers sing praise with me, and thou,[9] my Continence, sing praise my Righteousness by me; praise that which is righteous.

77. O Communion which is in me, praise the All.

78. By me the Truth sings praise to the Truth, the Good praiseth the Good.

79. O Life, O Light, from us, unto you, comes this praise and thanksgiving.

80. I give thanks unto thee, O Father, the operation or act of my Powers.

81. I give thanks unto thee, O God, the Power of my operations.

82. By me thy Word sings praise unto thee; receive by me this reasonable (or verbal) Sacrifice in words.

83. The powers that are in me cry these things, they praise the All, they fulfil thy Will; thy Will and Counsel is form thee unto thee.

84. O All, receive a reasonable Sacrifice from all things.

85. O Life, save all that is in us; O Light enlighten, O God, the Spirit; for the Mind guideth (or feedeth) the Word; O Spirit bearing Workman.

86. Thou are God, thy Man crieth these things unto thee through, by the Fire, by the Air, by the Earth, by the Water, by the Spirit, by thy Creatures.

87. From eternity I have found (means to) bless and praise thee, and I have what I seek, for I rest in thy Will.

88. Tat:—O Father, I see thou hast sung this Song of praise and blessing, with thy whole Will; and therefore have I put and placed it in my World.

89. Hermes:—Say in thy Intelligible World, O Son.

90. TAT:—I do mean in my Intelligible World, for by thy Hymn and Song of Praise my mind is enlightened, and gladly would I send from my Understanding, a Thanksgiving unto God.

91. HERMES:—Not rashly, O Son.

92. TAT:—In my Mind, O Father.

93. HERMES:—Those things that I see and contemplate, I infuse them into thee, and therefore say, thou Son, Tat, the Author of thy succeeding Generations, I send unto God these reasonable Sacrifices.

94. O God, Thou art the Father, Thou art the Lord, Thou art the Mind, accept these reasonable Sacrifices which Thou requirest of Me.

95. For all things are done as the Mind willeth.

96. Thou, O Son, send this acceptable Sacrifice to God, the Father of all things; but propound it also, O Son, by Word.

97. TAT:—I thank thee, Father, thou hast advised and instructed me thus to give praise and thanks.

98. HERMES:—I am glad, O Son, to see the Truth bring forth the Fruits of Good things, and such immortal Branches.

99. And learn this from me: Above all other Virtues entertain Silence, and impart unto no man, O Son, the tradition of Regeneration, lest we be reputed Calumniators; For we both have now sufficiently meditated, I in speaking, thou in hearing. And now thou dost intellectually know thyself and our Father.

THE END OF

## THE SEVENTH BOOK.

# THE EIGHTH BOOK,

CALLED

## "THAT THE GREATEST EVIL IN MAN, IS, THE NOT KNOWING GOD."

———

WHITHER are you carried, O Men, drunken with drinking strong Wine of Ignorance? Which seeing you cannot bear: Why do you vomit it up again?

2. Stand, and be sober, and look up again with the eyes of your Heart, and if you cannot all do so, yet do as many as you can.

3. For the malice of Ignorance surroundeth all the Earth, and corrupteth the Soul, shut up in the Body, not suffering it to arrive at the Havens of Salvation.

4. Suffer not yourselves to be carried with the Great Stream, but stem the tide, you that can lay hold of the Haven of Safety, and make your full course towards it.

5. Seek one that may lead you by the hand, and conduct you to the door of Truth and Knowledge, where the clear Light is that is pure from Darkness, where there is not one drunken, but all are sober, and in their heart look up to him, whose pleasure it is to be seen.

6. For he cannot be heard with ears, nor seen with eyes, nor expressed in words; but only in mind and heart.

7. But first thou must tear to pieces, and break through the garment thou wearest; the web of Ignorance, the foundation of all Mischief; the bond of Corruption; the dark Coverture;

the living Death; the sensible Carcass; the Sepulchre, carried about with us; the domestical Thief, which in what he loves us, hates us, envies us.

8. Such is the hurtful Apparel, wherewith thou art clothed, which draws and pulls thee downward by its own self; lest looking upward, and seeing the beauty of Truth, and the Good that is reposed therein, thou shouldst hate the wickedness of this Garment and understand the traps and ambushes, which it had laid for thee.

9. Therefore doth it labour to make good those things that seem, and are by the Senses, judged and determined; and the things that are truly, it hides, and envelopeth in such matter, filling what it presents unto thee, with hateful pleasure, that thou canst neither hear what thou shouldst hear, nor see what thou shouldst see.

THE END OF

THE EIGHTH BOOK.

# THE NINTH BOOK,

## "A UNIVERSAL SERMON TO ASCLEPIUS."

———

HERMES:—All that is moved, O Asclepius, is it not moved in something and by something?

2. ASCLEPIUS:—Yes, indeed.

3. HERMES:—Must not that, in which a thing is moved, of necessity be greater than the thing that is moved?

4. Of necessity.

5. And that which moveth, is it not stronger than that which is moved?

6. ASCLEPIUS:—It is stronger.

7. HERMES:—That in which a thing is moved, must it not needs have a Nature, contrary to that of the thing that is moved?

8. ASCLEPIUS:—It must needs.

9. HERMES:—Is not this great World a Body, than which there is no greater?

10. ASCLEPIUS:—Yes, confessedly.

11. HERMES:—And is it not solid, as filled with many great Bodies, and indeed, with all the Bodies that are?

12. ASCLEPIUS:—It is so.

13. HERMES:—And is not the World a Body, and a Body that is moved?

14. ASCLEPIUS:—It is.

15. HERMES:—Then what a kind of place must it be, wherein it is moved, and of what Nature? Must it not be much bigger, that it may receive the continuity of Motion? And lest which

is moved, should for want of room, be stayed, and hindered in the Motion?

16. ASCLEPIUS:—It must needs be an immense thing, Trismegistus, but of what Nature?

17. HERMES:—Of a contrary Nature, O Asclepius; but is not the Nature of things unbodily, contrary to a Body?

18. ASCLEPIUS:—Confessedly.

19. HERMES:—Therefore the place is unbodily; but that which is unbodily, is either some Divine thing, or God himself. And by something Divine, I do not mean that which was made or begotten.

20. If therefore it be Divine, it is an Essence or Substance; but if it be God, it is above Essence; but he is otherwise intelligible.

21. For the first, God is intelligible, not to himself, but to us; for that which is intelligible, is subject to that which understandeth by Sense.

22. Therefore, God is not intelligible to himself, for not being any other thing from that which is understood, he cannot be understood by himself.

23. But he is another thing from us, and therefore he is understood by us.

24. If therefore Place be intelligible, it is not Place but God, but if God be intelligible, he is intelligible not as Place, but as a capable Operation.

25. Now, everything that is moved, is moved, not in or by that which is moved, but in that which standeth or resteth, and that which moveth standeth or resteth, for it is impossible it should be moved with it.

26. ASCLEPIUS:—How, then, O Trismegistus, are those things that are here moved with the things that are moved? For thou sayest that the Spheres that wander, are moved by the Sphere that wanders not.

27. HERMES:—That, O Asclepius, is not a moving together, but a countermotion, for they are not moved after a like manner, but contrary one to the other; and contrariety hath a standing resistance of motion, for {the άυννπίκ, or} resistance is a staying of Motion.

28. Therefore, the wandering Spheres being moved contrarily to that Sphere which wandereth not, shall have one from another contrarily standing of itself.

29. For this Bear thou seest neither rise nor go down, but turning always about the same; dost thou think it moveth or standeth still?

30. ASCLEPIUS:—I think it moves, Trismegistus.

31. What motion, O Asclepius?

32. ASCLEPIUS:—A motion that is always carried about the same.

33. But the Circulation which is about the same, and the motion about the same, are both hidden by Station; for that which is about the same, forbids that which is above the same, if it stand to that which is about the same.

34. And so the contrary motion stands fast always, being always established by the contrariety.

35. But I will give thee concerning this matter, an Earthly example, that may be seen with eyes.

36. Look upon any of these living Creatures upon Earth, as Man, for example, and see him swimming; for as the Water is carried one way, the reluctation or resistance of his feet and hands is made a station to the Man, that he should not be carried with the Water, nor sink underneath it.

37. ASCLEPIUS:—Thou hast laid down a very clear example, Trismegistus.

38. HERMES:—Therefore, every motion is in station, and is moved of station.

39. The motion, then, of the World, and of every material living thing, happeneth not to be done by those things that

are without the World, but by those things within it, a Soul, or Spirit, or some other unbodily thing, to those things that are without it.

40. For an inanimate Body, doth not know, much less a Body if it be wholly inanimate.

41. Asclepius:—What meaneth thou by this, O Trismegistus, Wood and Stones, and all other inanimate things, are they not moving Bodies?

42. Hermes:—By no means, O Asclepius, for that within the Body, which moves the inanimate thing, is not the Body, that moves both as well the Body of that which beareth, as the Body of that which is born; for one dead or inanimate thing, cannot move another; that which moveth, must needs be alive if it move.

43. Thou seest therefore how the Soul is surcharged, when it carrieth two Bodies.

44. And now it is manifest, that the things that are moved in something, and by something.

45. Asclepius:—The things that are moved, O Trismegistus, must needs be moved in that which is void, or empty, a Vacuum{, κενόν}.

46. Be advised, O Asclepius, for all the things that are, there is nothing empty, only that which is not, is empty and a stranger to existence or being.

47. But that which is could not be if it were not full of existence, for that which is in being or existence can never be made empty.

48. Asclepius:—Are there not therefore some things that are empty, O Trismegistus, as an empty Barrel, an empty Hogshead, an empty Well, an empty Wine-Press, and many such like?

49. Hermes:—O the grossness of thy Error, O Asclepius; those things that are most full and replenished, dost thou account them void and empty?

50. ASCLEPIUS:—What may be thy meaning, Trismegistus?

51. HERMES:—Is not the Air a Body?

52. ASCLEPIUS:—It is a Body.

53. HERMES:—Why then this Body, doth it not pass through all things that are, and passing through them, fill them? And that Body, doth it not consist of the mixture of the four? Therefore, all those things which thou callest empty are full of Air.

54. Therefore, those things thou callest empty, thou oughtest to call them hollow, not empty, for they exist and are full of Air and Spirit.

55. ASCLEPIUS:—This reason is beyond all contradiction, O Trismegistus, but what shall we call the Place in which the whole Universe is moved?

56. HERMES:—Call it incorporeal, O Asclepius.

57. ASCLEPIUS:—What is that, incorporeal or unbodily?

58. HERMES:—The Mind and Reason, the whole, wholly comprehending itself, free from all Body, undeceivable, invisible, impassible from a Body itself, standing fast in itself, capable of all things, and that favour[10] of the things that are.

59. Whereof the Good, the Truth, the Archetypal Light, the Archetype of the Soul, are, as it were, Beams.

60. ASCLEPIUS:—Why, then, what is God?

61. HERMES:—That which is none of these things, yet is, and is the cause of Being to all; and every one of the things that are; for he left nothing destitute of Being.

62. And all things are made of things that are, and not of things that are not; for the things that are not, have not the nature to be able to be made; and again, the things that are, have not the nature never to be, or not to be at all.

63. ASCLEPIUS:—What dost thou then say at length, that God is?

64. HERMES:—God is not a Mind, but the Cause that the Mind is; not a Spirit, but the Cause that the Spirit is; not Light, but the Cause that Light is.

65. Therefore, we must worship God by these two Appellations, which are proper to him alone, and to no other.

66. For neither of all the other, which are called Gods, nor of Men, nor Demons, or Angels, can anyone be, though never so little, Good, save only God alone.

67. And this He is, and nothing else; but all other things are separable from the nature of Good.

68. For the Body and the Soul have no place that is capable of or can contain the Good.

69. For the greatness of Good, is as great as the Existence of all things, that are both bodily and unbodily, both sensible and intelligible.

70. This is the Good, even God.

71. See, therefore, that thou do not at any time, call ought else Good, for so thou shalt be impious, or any else God, but only the Good, for so thou shalt again be impious.

72. In Word it is often said by all men the Good, but all men do not understand what it is; but through Ignorance they call both the Gods, and some men, Good, that can never be, or be made so.

73. Therefore all the other Gods are honoured with the title or appellation of God, but God is the Good, not according to Heaven, but Nature.

74. For there is one Nature of God, even the Good, and one kind of them both, from whence are all kinds.

75. For he that is Good, is the giver of all things, and takes nothing; and, therefore, God gives all things, and receives nothing.

76. The other title and appellation, is the Father, because of his making all things; for it is the part of a Father to make.

77. Therefore, it hath been the greatest and most Religious care in this life, to them that are Wise, and well-minded, to beget children.

78. As likewise it is the greatest misfortune and impiety, for any to be separated from men, without children; and this man is punished after Death by the Demons, and the punishment is this: To have the Soul of this childless man, adjudged and condemned to a Body, that neither hath the nature of a man, nor of a woman, which is an accursed thing under the Sun.

79. Therefore, O Asclepius, never congratulate any man that is childless; but on the contrary pity his misfortune, knowing what punishment abides, and is prepared for him.

80. Let so many, and such manner of things, O Asclepius, be said as a certain precognition of all things in Nature.

The End of

## THE NINTH BOOK.

# THE TENTH BOOK,

CALLED

## "THE MIND TO HERMES."

———

FORBEAR thy Speech, O Hermes Trismegistus, and call to mind to those things that are said; but I will not delay to speak what comes into my mind, since many men have spoken many things, and those very different, concerning the Universe, and Good; but I have not learned the Truth.

2. Therefore, the Lord make it plain to me in this point; for I will believe thee only, for the manifestation of these things.

3. Then said the Mind how the case stands.

4. God and All.

5. God, Eternity, the World, Time, Generation.

6. God made Eternity, Eternity the World, the World Time, and Time Generation.

7. Of God, as it were, the Substance, is the Good, the Fair, Blessedness, Wisdom.

8. Of Eternity, Identity, or Selfness.

9. Of the World, Order.

10. Of Time, Change.

11. Of Generation, Life and Death.

12. But the Operation of God, is Mind and Soul.

13. Of Eternity, Permanence, or Long-lasting, and Immortality.

14. Of the World, Restitution, and Decay, or Destruction.

15. Of Time, Augmentation and Diminution.

16. And of Generation, Qualities.

17. Therefore, Eternity is in God.

18. The World in Eternity.

19. Time in the World.

20. And Generation in Time.

21. And Eternity standeth about God.

22. The World is moved in Eternity.

23. Time is determined in the World.

24. Generation is done in Time.

25. Therefore, the Spring and Fountain of all things is God.

26. The Substance Eternity.

27. The Matter is the World.

28. The Power of God is Eternity.

29. And the Work of Eternity, is the World not yet made, and yet ever made by Eternity.

30. Therefore, shall nothing be at any time destroyed, for Eternity is incorruptible.

31. Neither can anything perish, or be destroyed in the World, the World being contained and embraced by Eternity.

32. But what is the Wisdom of God? Even the Good and the Fair, and Blessedness, and every Virtue, and Eternity.

33. Eternity, therefore, put into the Matter Immortality and Everlastingness; for the Generation of that depends upon Eternity, even as Eternity doth of God.

34. For Generation and Time, in Heaven and in Earth, are of a double Nature; in Heaven they are unchangeable and incorruptible, but on Earth they are changeable and corruptible.

35. And the Soul of Eternity is God; and the Soul of the World, Eternity; and of the Earth, Heaven.

36. God is in the Mind, the Mind in the Soul, the Soul in the Matter, all things by Eternity.

37. All this Universal Body, in which are all Bodies, is full of Soul, the Soul full of Mind, the Mind full of God.

38. For within he fills them, and without he contains them, quickening the Universe.

39. Without, he quickens this perfect living thing the World, and within all living Creatures.

40. And above in Heaven he abides in Identity or Selfness, but below upon Earth he changeth Generation.

41. Eternity comprehendeth the World, either by Necessity, or Providence, or Nature.

42. And if any man shall think any other thing, it is God that actuateth, or operateth this All.

43. But the operation or Act of God, is Power insuperable, to which none may compare anything, either Humane or Divine.

44. Therefore, O Hermes, think none of these things below, or the things above, in any wise like unto God; for if thou dost, thou errest from the Truth.

45. For nothing can be like the unlike, and only, and One; nor mayest thou think, that he hath given of his Power to any other thing.

46. For who after him can make anything, either of Life, or Immortality; of Change or of Quality, and himself, what other things should he make?

47. For God is not idle, for then all things would be idle; for all things are full of God.

48. But there is not anywhere in the World, such a thing as Idleness; for Idleness is a name that implieth a thing void or empty, both of a Doer, and a thing done.

49. But all things must necessarily be made or done both always, and according to the nature of every place.

50. For he that maketh or doth, is in all things, yet not fastened or comprehended in anything; nor making or doing one thing, but all things.

51. For being an active or operating Power, and sufficient of himself for the things that are made, and the things that are made are under him.

52. Look upon, through me, the World is subject to thy sight, and understand exactly the Beauty thereof.

53. A Body immarcessible,[11] than the which, there is nothing more ancient, yet always vigorous and young.

54. See also the seven Worlds set over us, adorned with an everlasting Order, and filling Eternity, with a different course.

55. For all things are full of Light, but the Fire is nowhere.

56. For the friendship and commixture of contraries and unlike, become Light shining from the Act or Operation of God, the Father of all Good, the Prince of all Order, and the Ruler of the seven Worlds.

57. Look also upon the Moon, the forerunner of them all, the Instrument of Nature, and which changeth the Matter here below.

58. Behold the Earth, the middle of the Whole, the firm and stable Foundation of the Fair World, the Feeder, and Nurse of Earthly things.

59. Consider, moreover, how great the multitude is of immortal living things, and of mortal ones also; and see the Moon going about in the midst of both, to wit, of things immortal and mortal.

60. But all things are full of Soul, and all things are properly moved by it; some things about the Heaven, and some things about the Earth, and neither of those on the right hand to the left; nor those on the left hand to the right; nor those things that are above, downward; nor those things that are below, upwards.

61. And that all these things are made, O beloved Hermes, thou needst not learn of me.

62. For they are Bodies, and have a Soul, and are moved.

63. And that all these should come together into one, it is impossible without something, to gather them together.

64. Therefore, there must be some such ones, and he altogether One.

65. For seeing that the motions are divers, and many, and the Bodies not alike, and yet one ordered swiftness among them all; It is impossible there should be two or more Makers.

66. For one order is not kept by many.

67. But in the weaker, there would be jealousy of the stronger, and thence also Contentions.

68. And if there were one Maker, of mutable mortal living wights, he would desire also to make immortal ones, as he that were the Maker of immortal ones, would do to make mortal.

69. Moreover, also, if there were two, the Matter of being one, who should be chief, or have the disposing of the facture?

70. Or if both of them, which of them the greater part?

71. But think thus that every living Body hath its consistence of Matter and Soul; and of that which is immortal, and that which is mortal and unreasonable.

72. For all living Bodies have a Soul; and those things that are not living, are only matter by itself.

73. And the Soul likewise of itself drawing near her Maker, is the Cause of Life and Being, and Being the cause of Life is, after a manner, the cause of immortal things.

74. How then are mortal wights, other from immortal?

75. Or how cannot he make living wights, that causeth immortal things and immortality?

76. That there is some Body that doth these things it is apparent, and that he is also one, it is most manifest.

77. For there is one Soul, one Life, and one Matter.

78. Who is this? Who can it be, other than the One God?

79. For whom else can it benefit, to make living things, save only God alone?

80. There is therefore One God.

81. For it is a ridiculous thing to confess the World to be one Sun, one Moon, one Divinity; and yet to have, I know not how many gods.

82. He therefore being One, doth all things in many things.

83. And what great thing is it for God, to make Life, and Soul, and Immortality, and Change, when thyself dost so many things?

84. For thou both seest, speaketh, and hearest, smellest, tastest, and touchest, walkest, understandest, and breathest.

85. And it is not one that seeth, and another that heareth, and another that speaketh, and another that toucheth, and another that smelleth, and another that walketh, and another that understandeth, and another that breatheth; but One that doth all these things.

86. Yet neither can these things possibly be without God.

87. For as thou, if thou shouldest cease from doing these things, were not a living wight; so if God should cease from those, he were not (which is not lawful to say) any longer God.

88. For if it be already demonstrated, that nothing can be idle or empty, how much more may be affirmed of God?

89. For if there be anything which he doth not do, then is he (if it were lawful to say so) imperfect.

90. Whereas, feeling[12] he is not idle, but perfect, certainly he doth all things.

91. Now give thyself unto me, O Hermes, for a little while, thou shalt the more easily understand, that it is the necessary work of God, that all things should be made or done that are done, or were once done, or shall be done.

92. And this, O best Beloved, is Life.

93. And this is the Fair.

94. And this is the Good.

95. And this is God.

96. And if thou wilt understand this by work also, mark what happens to thyself, when thou wilt generate.

97. And yet this is not like unto him; for he is not sensible of pleasure, for neither hath he any other Fellow Workman.

98. But being himself the only Workman, he is always in the Work, himself being that which he doth or maketh.

99. For all things, if they were separate from him, must needs fall and die, as there being no life in them.

100. And again, if all things be living wights, both which are in Heaven, and upon Earth; and that there be one Life in all things which are made by God, and that is God, then certainly all things are made, or done by God.

101. Life is the union of the Mind and the Soul.

102. But death is not the destruction of those things that were gathered together, but a dissolving of the Union.

103. The Image therefore of God, is Eternity; of Eternity, the World; of the World, the Sun: of the Sun, Man.

104. But the people say, That changing is Death, because the Body is dissolved, and the Life goeth into that which appeareth not.

105. By this discourse, my dearest Hermes, I affirm as thou hearest, That the World is changed, because every day part thereof becomes invisible; but that it is never dissolved.

106. And these are the Passions of the World, Revolutions and Occultations, and Revolution is a turning, but Occultation is Renovation.

107. And the World being all formed, hath not the forms lying without it, but itself changeth in itself.

108. Seeing then the World is all formed, what must he be that made it? For without form, he cannot be.

109. And if he be all formed, he will be kept like the World, but if he have but one form, he shall be in this regardless of the world.

110. What do we then say that he is? We will not raise any doubts by our speech; for nothing that is doubtful concerning God, is yet known.

111. He hath therefore one Idea, which is proper to him,

which, because it is unbodily, is not subject to the sight, and yet shews all forms by the Bodies.

112. And do not wonder, if there be an incorruptible Idea.

113. For they are like the Margents of the Speech, which is in writing; for they seem to be high and swelling, but they are by nature smooth and even.

114. But understand well this that I say, more boldly, for it is more true; As man cannot live without life, so neither can God live, not doing good.

115. For this is, as it were, the Life, and Motion of God, to move all things, and quicken them.

116. But some of the things I have said, must have a particular explanation; Understand then what I say.

117. All things are in God, not as lying in a place; for Place is both a Body, and unmoveable, and those things that are there placed, have no motion.

118. For they lie otherwise in that which is unbodily, than in the fantasy, or to appearance.

119. Consider him that contains all things, and understand, that nothing is more capacious, than that which is incorporeal, nothing more swift, nothing more powerful, but it is most capacious, most swift, and most strong.

120. And judge of this by thyself, command thy Soul to go into India, and sooner than thou canst bid it, it will be there.

121. Bid it likewise pass over the Ocean, and suddenly it will be there; Not as passing from place to place, but suddenly it will be there.

122. Command it to fly into Heaven, and it will need no Wings, neither shall anything hinder it; not the fire of the Sun, not the Aether, not the turning of the Spheres, not the Bodies of any other Stars, but cutting through all, it will fly up to the last, and furthest Body.

123. And if thou wilt even break the whole, and see those

things that are without the World (if there be anything without), thou mayest.

124. Behold, how great power, how great swiftness thou hast! Canst thou do all these things, and cannot God?

125. After this manner, therefore, contemplate God to have all the whole World to himself, as it were, all thoughts, or intellections.

126. If therefore thou wilt not equal thyself to God, thou canst not understand God.

127. For the like is intelligible by the like.

128. Increase thyself into an immeasureable greatness, leaping beyond every Body; and transcending all Time, become Eternity, and thou shalt understand God: If thou believe in thyself, that nothing is impossible, but accountest thyself immortal, and that thou canst understand all things, every Art, every Science, and the manner and custom of every living thing.

129. Become higher than all height, lower than all depths, comprehend in thyself, the qualities of all the Creatures, of the Fire, the Water, the Dry, and Moist; and conceive likewise, that thou canst at once be everywhere, in the Sea, in the Earth.

130. Thou shalt at once understand thyself, not yet begotten in the Womb, young, old, to be dead, the things after death, and all these together, as also times, places, deeds, qualities, quantities, or else thou canst not yet understand God.

131. But if thou shut up thy Soul in the Body, and abuse it, and say, I understand nothing, I can do nothing, I am afraid of the Sea, I cannot climb up into Heaven, I know not who I am, I cannot tell what I shall be; what hast thou to do with God? For thou canst understand none of those Fair and Good things; and be a lover of the Body, and Evil.

132. For it is the greatest Evil, not to know God.

133. But to be able to know, and to will, and to hope, is the straightway, and Divine way, proper to the Good; and it will everywhere meet thee, and everywhere be seen of thee, plain

and easy, when thou dost not expect or look for it; it will meet thee, waking, sleeping, sailing, travelling, by night, by day, when thou speakest, and when thou keepest silence.

134. For there is nothing which is not the Image of God.

135. And yet thou sayest, God is invisible; but be advised, for who is more manifest than He?

136. For therefore hath he made all things, that thou by all things mayest see Him.

137. This is the Good of God, this is the Virtue, to appear, and to be seen in all things.

138. There is nothing invisible, no, not of those things that are incorporeal.

139. The Mind is seen in Understanding, and God is seen in doing or making.

140. Let these things thus far forth, be made manifest unto thee, O Trismegistus.

141. Understand in like manner, all other things by thyself, and thou shalt not be deceived.

THE END OF

THE TENTH BOOK.

# THE ELEVENTH BOOK,

## "OF THE COMMON MIND, TO TAT."

————

The Mind, O Tat, is of the very Essence of God, if yet there be any Essence of God.

2. What kind of Essence that is, he alone knows himself exactly.

3. The Mind therefore is not cut off, or divided from the essentiality of God, but united as the light of the Sun.

4. And this Mind in men, is God, and therefore are some men Divine, and their Humanity is near Divinity.

5. For the good Demon called the Gods, immortal men, and men mortal Gods.

6. But in the Brute Beast, or unreasonable living wights, the Mind is their Nature.

7. For where there is a Soul, there is the Mind, as where there is Life, there is also a Soul.

8. In living Creatures, therefore, that are without Reason, the Soul is Life, void of the operations of the Mind.

9. For the Mind is the Benefactor of the Souls of men, and worketh to the proper Good.

10. And in unreasonable things it co-operateth with the Nature of every one of them, but in men it worketh against their Natures.

11. For the Soul being in the Body, is straightway made Evil by Sorrow, and Grief, and Pleasure, or Delight.

12. For Grief and Pleasure, flow like Juices from the compound Body, whereinto, when the Soul entereth, or descendeth, she is moistened and tincted with them.

13. As many Souls, therefore, as the Mind governeth, or over-ruleth, to them it shows its own Light, resisting their prepossessions or presumptions.

14. As a good Physician grieveth the Body, prepossessed of a disease, by burning or lancing it for health's sake.

15. After the same manner also, the Mind grieveth the Soul, by drawing it out of Pleasure, from whence every disease of the Soul proceedeth.

16. But the great Disease of the Soul is Atheism, because that opinion followeth to all Evil, and no Good.

17. Therefore, the Mind resisting, it procureth Good to the Soul, as a Physician health to the Body.

18. But as many Souls of Men, as do not admit or entertain the Mind for their Governor, do suffer the same thing that the Soul of unreasonable living things.

19. For the Soul being a Co-Operator with them, permits or leaves them to their concupiscences, whereunto they are carried by the torrent of their Appetite, and so tend to brutishness.

20. And as Brute Bests, they are angry without reason, and they desire without reason, and never cease, nor are satisfied with Evil.

21. For unreasonable Angers, and Desires are the most exceeding Evils.

22. And therefore hath God set the Mind over there, as a Revenger, and Reprover of them.

23. TAT:—Here, O Father, that discourse of Fate or Destiny, which thou madest to me, is in danger to be[13] overthrown; For if it be fatal for any man to commit Adultery or Sacrilege, or do any Evil, he is punished also, though he, of necessity, do the work of the Fate or Destiny.

24. HERMES:—All things, O Son, are the work of Fate, and without it, can no bodily thing, either Good or Evil, be done.

25. For it is decreed by Fate, that he that doth any Evil, should also suffer for it.

26. And therefore he doth it, that he may suffer that which he suffereth, because he did it.

27. But for the present, let alone that speech, concerning Evil and Fate, for at other times we have spoken of it.

28. Now, our discourse is about the Mind, and what it can do, and how it differs, and is in men such a one, but in Brute Beasts changed.

29. And again, in Brute Beasts it is not beneficial, but in men by quenching both their Anger, and Concupiscences.

30. And of men, thou must understand, some to be rational, or governed by reason, and some irrational.

31. But all men are subject to Fate, and to Generation, and Change, for these are the beginning and end of Fate or Destiny

32. And all men suffer those things that are decreed by Fate.

33. But rational men, over whom, as we said, the Mind bears rule, do not suffer like unto other men; but being free from viciousness, and being not Evil, they do suffer Evil.

34. TAT:—How sayest thou this again, Father? An Adulterer, is he not Evil? A Murderer, is he not Evil? And so all others.

35. HERMES:—But the rational man, O Son, will not suffer for Adultery, but as the Adulterer not for Murder, but as the Murderer.

36. And it is impossible to escape the Quality of Change, as of Generation, but the Viciousness, he that hath the Mind, may escape.

37. And therefore, O Son, I have always heard the good Demon say, and if he had delivered it in writing, he had much profited all mankind: For he alone, O Son, as the first born, God, seeing all things, truly spake Divine words. I have heard him sometimes, That all Things are one thing, Especially

Intelligible Bodies, or that all Especially Intelligible Bodies are one.

38. We live in Power, in Act, and in Eternity.

39. Therefore, a good Mind, is that which the Soul of him is.

40. And if this be so, then no intelligible thing differs from intelligible things.

41. As, therefore, it is possible that the Mind, the Prince of all things; so likewise, that the Soul that is of God, can do whatsoever it will.

42. But understand thou well, for this Discourse I have made to the Question which thou askest of me before, I mean concerning Fate and the Mind.

43. First, if, O Son, thou shalt diligently withdraw thyself from all Contentious speeches, thou shalt find that in Truth, the Mind, the Soul of God bears rule over all things, both over Fate, and Law, and all other things.

44. And nothing is impossible to him, no, not of the things that are of Fate.

45. Therefore, though the Soul of Man be above it, let it not neglect the things that happen to be under Fate.

46. And these, thus far, were the excellent sayings of the good Demon.

47. Tat:—Most divinely spoken, O Father, and truly and profitably, yet clear this one thing unto me.

48. Thou sayest, that in Brute Beasts the Mind worketh or acteth after the manner of Nature, co-operating also with their ({ὁρμάς,} impetus) inclinations.

49. Now, the impetuous inclinations of Brute Beasts, as I conceive, are Passions. If, therefore, the Mind do co-operate with these impetuous Inclinations, and that they are the Passions in Brute Beasts, certainly the Mind is also a Passion, conforming itself to Passions.

50. Hermes:—Well done, Son, thou askest nobly, and yet it is just that I should answer thee.

51. All incorporeal things, O Son, that are in the Body, are passible, nay, they are properly Passions.

52. Everything that moveth is incorporeal; everything that is moved is a Body; and it is moved into the Bodies by the Mind. Now, Motion is Passion, and there they both suffer; as well that which moveth, as that which is moved, as well that which ruleth, as that which is ruled.

53. But being freed from the Body, it is freed likewise from Passion.

54. But especially, O Son, there is nothing impassible, but all things are passible.

55. But Passion differs from that which is passible; for that (Passion) acteth, but this suffers.

56. Bodies also of themselves do act, for either they are unmoveable, or else are moved; and which soever it be, it is a Passion.

57. But incorporeal things do always act, or work, and therefore they are passible.

58. Let not, therefore, the appellations or names trouble thee, for Action and Passion are the same thing, but that it is not grievous to use the more honourable name.

59. TAT:—O Father, thou hast delivered this Discourse most plainly.

60. HERMES:—Consider this also, O Son, That God hath freely bestowed upon man, above all other living things, these two, to wit, Mind and Speech, or Reason, {λόγος,} equal to immortality.

61. These, if any man use, or employ upon what he ought, he shall differ nothing from the Immortals.

62. Yea, rather going out of the Body, he shall be guided and led by them, both into the Choir and Society of the God, and blessed Ones.

63. TAT:—Do not other living Creatures use Speech, O Father?

64. HERMES:—No, Son, but only Voice; now, Speech and Voice do differ exceeding much; for Speech is common to all men, but Voice is proper unto every kind of living thing.

65. TAT:—Yea, but the Speech of men is different, O Father, every man according to his Nation.

66. HERMES:—It is true, O Son, they do differ: Yet as man is one, so is Speech one also; and it is interpreted and found the same, both in Egypt, Persia, and Greece.

67. But thou seemest unto me, Son, to be ignorant of the Virtue, or Power and Greatness of Speech.

68. For the blessed God, the good Demon said or commanded the Soul to be in the Body, the Mind, in the Soul, {(χόγος)} the Word, or Speech, or Reason in the Mind, and the Mind in God, and that God is the Father of them all.

69. Therefore, the Word is the Image of the Mind, and the Mind of God, and the Body of the Idea, and the Idea of the Soul.

70. Therefore, of the Matter, the subtlest or smallest part is Air, of the Air the Soul, of the Soul the Mind, of the Mind God.

71. And God is about all things, and through all things, but the Mind about the Soul, the Soul about the Air, and the Air about the Matter.

72. But Necessity, and Providence, and Nature, are the Organs or Instruments of the World, and of the Order of Matter.

73. For of those things that are intelligible, everyone is, but the Essence of them is Identity.

74. But of the Bodies of the whole, or universe, everyone is many things.

75. For the Bodies that are put together, and that have, and make their changes into other, having this Identity, do always and preserve the incorruption of the Identity.

76. But in every one of the compound Bodies there is a Number

77. For without Number it is impossible there should be consistence or constitution, or composition, or dissolution.

78. But Unities do both beget and increase Numbers, and again being dissolved, come into themselves.

79. And the Matter is One.

80. But this whole World, the great God, and the Image of the Greater, and united unto him, and concerning the Order, and Will of the Father, is the fulness of Life.

81. And there is nothing therein, through all the Eternity of the Revolutions, neither of the whole, nor of the parts which doth not live.

82. For there is nothing dead, that either hath been, or is, or shall be in the World.

83. For the Father would have it, as long as it lasts, to be a living thing; and therefore it must needs be God also.

84. How, therefore, O Son, can there be in God in the image of the Universe, in the fulness of Life, any dead things?

85. For dying is corruption, and corruption is destruction.

86. How, then, can any part of the incorruptible be corrupted, or of God be destroyed?

87. TAT:—Therefore, O Father, do not the living things in the World die, though they be parts thereof?

88. HERMES:—Be wary in thy Speech, O Son, and not deceived in the names of things.

89. For they do not die, O Son, but as compound Bodies they are dissolved.

90. But dissolution is not death; and they are dissolved, not that they may be destroyed, but that they may be made new.

91. TAT:—What, then, is the Operation of Life? Is it not Motion?

92. HERMES:—And what is there in the World unmoveable? Nothing at all, O Son.

93. TAT:—Why, doth not the Earth seem immoveable to thee, O Father?

94. HERMES:—No, but subject to many Motions, though after a manner, it alone be stable.

95. What a ridiculous thing it were, that the Nurse of all things should be immoveable, which beareth and bringeth forth all things.

96. For it is impossible, that anything that bringeth forth, should bring forth without Motion.

97. And a ridiculous question it is, Whether the fourth part of the whole, be idle: For the word immoveable, or without Motion, signifies nothing else, but idleness.

98. Know generally, O Son, That whatsoever is in the World is moved either according to Augmentation or Diminution.

99. But that which is moved, liveth also, yet it is not necessary, that a living thing should be or continue the same.

100. For while the whole World is together, it is unchangeable, O Son, but all the parts thereof are changeable.

101. Yet nothing is corrupted or destroyed, and quite abolished, but the names trouble men.

102. For Generation is not Life, but Sense; neither is Change Death, but Forgetfulness, or rather Occultation, and lying hid. Or better thus:—

For Generation is not a Creation of Life, but a Production of Things to Sense, and making them Manifest. Neither is Change Death, but an Occultation of Hiding of that which was.

103. These things being so, all things are Immortal, Matter, Life, Spirit, Soul, Mind, whereof every living thing consisteth.

104. Every living thing therefore is Immortal, because of the Mind, but especially Man, who both receiveth God, and converseth with him.

105. For with this living wight, alone is God familiar; in the night by dreams, in the day by Symbols or Signs.

106. And by all things doth he foretell him of things to come, by Birds, by Fowls, by the Spirit, or Wind, and by an Oak.

107. Wherefore, also, Man professeth to know things that have been, things that are present, and things to come.

108. Consider this also, O Son, That every other living Creature goeth upon one part of the World, Swimming things in the Water, Land wights upon the Earth, Flying Fowls in the Air.

109. But Man useth all these, the Earth, the Water, the Air, and the Fire, nay, he seeth and toucheth Heaven by his Senses.

110. But God is both about all things, and through all things, for he is both Act and Power.

111. And it is no hard thing, O Son, to understand God.

112. And if thou wilt also see him, look upon the Necessity of things that appear, and the Providence of things that have been, and are done.

113. See the Matter being most full of Life, and so great a God moved, with all Good, and Fair, both Gods, and Demons, and Men.

114. TAT:—But these, O Father, are wholly Acts, or Operations.

115. HERMES:—If they be, therefore, wholly Acts or Operations, O Son, by whom are they acted or operated, but by God?

116. Or art thou ignorant, that as parts of the World, are Heaven, and Earth, and Water, and Air; after the same manner, the Members of God, are Life, and Immortality, and Eternity, and Spirit, and Necessity, and Providence, and Nature, and Soul, and Mind, and the Continuance or Perseverance of all these which is called Good.

117. And there is not anything of all that hath been, and all that is, where God is not.

118. TAT:—What, in Matter, O Father?

119. HERMES:—The Matter, Son, what is it without God, that thou shouldst ascribe a proper place to it?

120. Or what dost thou think it to be? Peradventure, some heap that is not actuated or operated.

121. But if it be actuated, by whom is it actuated? For we have said, that Acts or Operations, are the parts of God.

122. By whom are all living things quickened? And the Immortal, by whom are they immortalized? The things that are changeable, by whom are they changed?

123. Whether thou speak of Matter, or Body, or Essence, know that all these are Acts of God.

124. And that the Act of Matter is materiality, and of the Bodies corporality, and of Essence essentiality; and this is God the whole.

125. And in the whole, there is nothing that is not God.

126. Wherefore, about God, there is neither Greatness, Place, Quality, Figure, or Time; for he is All, and the All, through all, and about all.

127. This Word, O Son, worship and adore. And the only service of God, is not to be Evil.

THE END OF

## THE ELEVENTH BOOK.

# THE TWELFTH BOOK,

## CALLED

## "HIS CRATER OR MONAS."

------

THE Workman made this Universal World, not with his Hands, but his Word.

2. Therefore thus think of him, as present everywhere, and being always, and making all things, and one above, that by his Will hath framed the things that are.

3. For that is his Body, not tangible, nor visible, nor measurable, nor extensible, nor like any other Body.

4. For it is neither Fire, nor Water, nor Air, nor Wind, but all these things are of him; for being Good, he hath dedicated that name unto himself alone.

5. But he would also adorn the Earth, but with the Ornament of a Divine Body.

6. And he sent Man, an Immortal, and a Mortal wight.

7. And Man had more than all living Creatures, and the World, because of his Speech, and Mind.

8. For Man became the Spectator of the Works of God, and wondered, and acknowledged the Maker.

9. For he divided Speech among all men, but not Mind, and yet he envied not any; for Envy comes not thither, but is abode here below in the Souls of men, that have not the Mind.

10. TAT:—But wherefore, Father, did not God distribute the Mind to all men?

11. HERMES:—Because it pleased him, O Son, to set that in the middle among all souls, as a reward to strive for.

12. Tat:—And where hath he set it?

13. Hermes:—Filling a large Cup or Bowl therewith, he sent it down, giving also a Cryer or Proclaimer.

14. And he commanded him to proclaim these things to the souls of men.

15. Dip and wash thyself, thou that art able, in this Cup or Bowl; Thou that believest, that thou shalt return to him that sent this Cup; thou that acknowledgest whereunto thou wert made.

16. As many, therefore, as understood the Proclamation, and were baptized, or dowsed into the Mind, these were made partakers of Knowledge, and became perfect men, receiving the Mind.

17. But as many as missed of the Proclamation, they received Speech, but not Mind, being ignorant whereunto they were made, or by whom.

18. But their Senses are just like to Brute Beasts, and having their temper in Anger and Wrath, they do not admire the things worthy of looking on.

19. But wholly addicted to the pleasures and desires of the Bodies, they believe that man was made for them.

20. But as many as partook of the gift of God, these, O Tat, in comparison of their works, are rather immortal, than mortal men.

21. Comprehending all things in their Mind, which are upon Earth, which are in Heaven, and if there be anything above Heaven.

22. And lifting up themselves so high, they see the Good, and seeing it, they account it a miserable calamity to make their abode here.

23. And despising all things bodily and unbodily, they make haste to the One and Only.

24. Thus, O Tat, is the Knowledge of the Mind, the beholding of Divine Things, and the Understanding of God,

the Cup itself, being Divine.

25. Tat:—And I, O Father, would be baptized and drenched therein.

26. Hermes:—Except thou first hate thy Body, O Son, thou canst not love thyself; but loving thyself, thou shalt have the Mind, and having the Mind, thou shalt also partake the Knowledge or Science.

27. Tat:—How meanest thou that, O Father?

28. Hermes:—Because it is impossible, O Son, to be conversant about things Mortal and Divine.

29. For the things that are, being two Bodies, and things incorporeal, wherein is the Mortal and the Divine, the Election or Choice of either is left to him that will choose; For no man can choose both.

30. And of which soever the choice is made, the other being diminished or overcome, magnifieth the Act or Operation of the other.

31. The choice of the better, therefore, is not only best for him that chooseth it, by deifying man; but it also shewth Piety and Religion towards God.

32. But the choice of the worst destroys a man, but doth nothing against God; save that as Pomps or Pageants, when they come abroad, cannot do anything themselves, but hinder; after the same manner also do these make Pomps and Pageants in the World, being seduced by the pleasures of the Body.

33. These Things being so, O Tat, that things have been, and are so plenteously ministered to us from God; let them proceed also from us, without any scarcity or sparing.

34. For God is innocent or guiltless, but we are the causes of Evil, preferring them before the Good.

35. Thou seest, O Son, how many Bodies we must go beyond, and how many Choirs of Demons, and what continuity and courses of Stars, that we may make haste to the One, and only God.

36. For the Good is not to be transcended, it is unbounded and infinite; unto itself, without beginning, but unto us, seeming to have a beginning, even our knowledge of it.

37. For our Knowledge is not the beginning of it, but shews us the beginning of its being known unto us.

38. Let us, therefore, lay hold of the beginning, and we shall quickly go through all things.

39. It is indeed a difficult thing, to leave those things that are accustomable, and present, and turn us to those things that are ancient, and according to the original.

40. For these things that appear, delight us, but make the things that appear not, hard to believe, or the Things that Appear not, are Hard to believe.

41. The things most apparent are Evil, but the Good is secret, or hid in, or to the things that appear; for it hath neither Form nor Figure.

42. For this cause it is like to itself, but unlike everything else; for it is impossible, that anything incorporeal, should be made know, or appear to a Body.

43. For this is the difference between the like and the unlike, and the unlike wanteth always somewhat of the like.

44. For the Unity, Beginning, and Root of all things, as being the Root and Beginning.

45. Nothing is without a beginning, but the Beginning is of nothing, but of itself; for it is the Beginning of all other things.

46. Therefore it is, seeing it is not from another beginning.

47. Unity therefore being the Beginning, containeth very number, but itself is contained of none, and begetteth every number, itself being begotten of no other number.

48. Everything that is begotten (or made), is imperfect, and may be divided, increased, diminished.

49. But to the perfect, there happeneth none of these.

50. And that which is increased, is increased by Unity, but is consumed and vanished through weakness, being not able to receive the Unity.

51. This Image of God, have I described to thee, O Tat, as well as I could; which if thou do diligently consider, and view by the eyes of thy Mind, and heart, believe me, Son, thou shalt find the way to things above, or, rather, the Image itself will lead thee.

52. But the spectacle or sight, hath this peculiar and proper; Them that can see, and behold it, it holds fast and draws unto it, as they say, the Loadstone doth Iron.

THE END OF

## THE TWELFTH BOOK.

# THE THIRTEENTH BOOK,

## "OF SENSE AND UNDERSTANDING."

———

YESTERDAY, Asclepius, I delivered a perfect Discourse; but now I think it necessary, in suite of that, to dispute also of Sense.

2. For Sense and Understanding seem to differ, because the one is material, and the other essential.

3. But unto me, they appear to be both one, or united, and not divided in men, I mean.

4. For in other living Creatures, Sense is united unto Nature, but in men to Understanding.

5. But the Mind differs from Understanding, as much as God from Divinity.

6. For Divinity is {(ὑπό)} from or under God, and Understanding from the Mind, being the Sister of the Word or Speech, and they the Instruments one of another.

7. For neither is the Word pronounced without Understanding, neither is Understanding manifested without the Word.

8. Therefore, Sense and Understanding do both flow together into a man, as if they were infolded one within another.

9. For neither is it possible without Sense to Understand, nor can we have Sense without Understanding.

10. And yet it is possible (for the Time being), that the Understanding may understand without Sense, as they that fancy Visions in their Dreams.

11. But it seems unto me, that both the operations are in

the Visions of Dreams, and that the Sense is stirred up out of sleep, into awakening.

12. For Man is divided into a Body, and a Soul; when both parts of the Sense accord one with another, then is the Understanding childed, or brought forth by the Mind pronounced.

13. For the Mind brings forth all Intellections or Understandings. Good ones when it receiveth good Seed from God; and the contrary, when it receives them from Devils.

14. For there is not part of the World void of the Devil, which entering in privately, sowed the seed of his own proper operation; and the Mind did make pregnant, or did bring forth that which was sown. Adulteries, Murders, Striking of Parents, Sacrileges, Impieties, Stranglings, throwing down headlong, and all other things, which are the works of Evil Demons.

15. And the Seeds of God are few, but Great, and Fair, and Good; Virtue, and Temperance, and Piety.

16. And the Piety is the Knowledge of God, whom whosoever knoweth, being full of all good things, hath Divine Understanding, and not like the Many.

17. And therefore they that have that Knowledge, neither please the multitude, nor the multitude them, but they seem to be mad, and to move laughter, hated and despised, and many times also murdered.

18. For we have already said, That wickedness must dwell here, being in her own region.

19. For her region is the Earth, and not the World, as some will sometimes say, Blaspheming.

20. But the Godly or God-worshipping Man, laying hold on Knowledge, will despise or tread under all these things; for though they be evil to other men, yet to him all things are good.

21. And upon mature consideration, he refers all things to Knowledge, and that which is most to be wondered at, he alone makes Evil things Good.

22. But I return again to my Discourse of Sense.

23. It is, therefore, a thing proper to Man, to communicate, and conjoin Sense, and Understanding.

24. But every man, as I said before, doth not enjoy Understanding; for one man is material, another Essential.

25. And he that is material with wickedness, as I said, received from the Devils the Seed of Understanding; but they that are with the Good essentially, are saved[14] with God.

26. For God is the Workman of all things; and when he worketh, he useth Nature.

27. He maketh all things Good like himself.

28. But these things that are made Good, are in the use of Operation, unlawful.

29. For the Motion of the World, stirring up Generations, makes Qualities, infesting some with evilness, and purifying some with Good.

30. And the World, Asclepius, hath a peculiar Sense and Understanding, not like to Man's, nor so various or manifold, but a better and more simple.

31. For the Sense and Understanding of the World is One, in that it makes all things, and unmakes them again into itself; for it is the Organ of Instrument of the Will of God.

32. And it is so organized or framed, and made for an Instrument by God; that receiving all Seeds into itself from God, and keeping them in itself, it maketh all things effectually, and dissolving them, reneweth all things.

33. And therefore like a good Husband-man of Life, when things are dissolved or loosened, he affords, by the casting of Seed, renovation to all things that grow.

34. There is nothing that it (the World) doth not beget or bring forth alive; and by its Motion, it makes all things alive.

35. And it is at once, both the Place and the Workman of Life.

36. But the Bodies are from the Matter, in a different

manner; for some are of Earth, some of Water, some of Air, some of Fire, and all are compounded, but some are more compounded, and some are more simple.

37. They that are compounded, are the heavier, and they that are less, are the higher.

38. And the swiftness of the Motion of the World, makes the varieties of the Qualities of Generation, for the Spiration of Influence, being most frequent, extendeth unto the Bodies' qualities, with one fulness, which is of Life.

39. Therefore, God is the Father of the World, but the World is the Father of things in the World.

40. And the World is the Son of God, but things in the World, are the Sons of the World.

41. And, therefore, it is well called {κόσμος,} the World, that is, an Ornament, because it adorneth, and beautifieth all things with the variety of Generation, and indeficiency of Life, which the unweariedness of Operation, and the swiftness of Necessity, with the mingling of Elements, and the order of things done.

42. Therefore, it is necessarily, and proper called {κόσμος,} the World.

43. For all living things, both the Sense, and the Understanding, cometh into them from without, inspired by that which compasseth them about, and continueth them.

44. And the World receiving it once from God as soon as it was made, hath it still, What Ever it Once Had.

45. But God is not as it seems to some who Blaspheme through superstition, without Sense, and without Mind, or Understanding.

46. For all things that are, O Asclepius, are in God, and made by him, and depend of him, some working by Bodies, some moving by a Soul-like Essence, some quickening by a Spirit, and some receiving the things that are weary, and all very fitly.

47. Or rather, I say, that he hath them not, but I declare the Truth, He is All Things, not receiving them from without, but exhibiting them outwardly.

48. And this is the Sense, and Understanding of God, to move all things always.

49. And there shall never be any time, when any of these things that are, shall fail, or be wanting.

50. When I say the things that are, I mean God, for the things that are, God hath; and neither is there anything without him, nor he without anything.

51. These things, O Asclepius, will appear to be true, if thou understand them, but if thou understand them not, incredible.

52. For to understand, is to believe, but not to believe, is not to understand; For my Speech or Words reach not unto the Truth, but the Mind is great, and being led or conducted for a while by Speech, is able to attain to the Truth.

53. And understanding all things round about, and finding them consonant, and agreeable to those things that were delivered, and interrupted by Speech, believeth; and in that Good belief, resteth.

54. To them, therefore, that understand the things that have been said of God, they are credible, but to them that understand them not, incredible.

55. And let these, and thus many things, be spoken concerning Understanding, and Sense.

THE END OF

THE THIRTEENTH BOOK.

# THE FOURTEENTH BOOK,

## "OF OPERATION AND SENSE."

————

Tat:—Thou has well explained these things, Father. Teach me furthermore these things, for thou sayest, that Science and Art were the operations of the Rational, but now thou sayest, that Beasts are unreasonable, and for want of Reason, both are, and are called Brutes, so that by this reason, it must needs follow, that unreasonable Creatures partake not of Science, or Art, because they come short of Reason.

2. Hermes:—It must needs be so, Son.

3. Tat:—Why then, O Father, do we see some unreasonable living Creatures use both Science and Art; as the Pismires treasure up for themselves food against Winter, and Fowls of the Air likewise make them Nests, and four-footed Beasts know their own Dens?

4. These things they do, O Son, not by Science or Art, but by Nature; For Science and Art are things that are taught, but none of these Brute Beasts are taught any of these things.

5. But these things being Natural unto them, are wrought by Nature, whereas, Art, and Science do not happen unto all, but unto some.

6. As Men are Musicians, but not all; neither are all Archers, or Huntsmen, or the rest, but some of them have learned something by the working of Science, or Art.

7. After the same manner also, if some Pismires did so,

and some not, thou mightest well say, they gather their Food according to Science, and Art.

8. But seeing,[15] they are all led by Nature, to the same thing, even against their Wills, it is manifest they do not do it by Science or Art.

9. For Operations, O Tat, being unbodily, are in Bodies, and work by bodies.

10. Wherefore, O Tat, in as much as they are unbodily, thou must needs say, they are immortal.

11. But inasmuch as they cannot act without Bodies, I say, they are always in a Body.

12. For those things that are to anything, or for the cause of anything made subject to Providence or Necessity, cannot possibly remain idle of their own proper operation.

13. For that which is, shall ever be; for both the Body, and the Life of it, is the same.

14. And by this reason, it follows, that the Bodies also are always, because I affirm: That this corporeity is always by the Act, and Operation, or for them.

15. For although Earthly Bodies be subject to dissolution; yet these Bodies must be the Places, and the Organs, and Instruments of Acts or Operations.

16. But Acts or Operations are Immortal, and that which is Immortal, is always in Act, and therefore also Corporification if it be always.

17. Acts or Operations do follow the Soul, yet come not suddenly or promiscuously, but some of them come together with being made man, being about brutish or unreasonable things.

18. But the purer Operations do insensibly in the change of time, work with the oblique part of the Soul.

19. And these Operations depend upon Bodies; and truly they that are Corporifying, come from the Divine Bodies into Mortal ones.

20. But every one of them acteth both about the Body and the Soul, and are present with the Soul, even without the Body.

21. And they are always Acts or Operations, but the Soul is not always in a Mortal Body, for it can be without a Body, but Acts or Operations cannot be without Bodies.

22. This is a sacred Speech, Son, the Body cannot Consist without a Soul.

23. Tat:—How meanest thou that, Father?

24. Hermes:—Understand it thus, O Tat, When the Soul is separated from the Body, there remaineth that same body.

25. And this same Body, according to the time of its abode, is actuated, or operated in that it is dissolved and becomes invisible.

26. And these things the Body cannot suffer without Act or Operation, and consequently there remaineth with the Body, the same Act or Operation.

27. This then is the difference between an Immortal Body, and a Mortal one, that the Immortal one consists of one Matter, and so doth not the Mortal one; and the Immortal one doth, but this suffereth.

28. And everything that Acteth or Operateth is stronger, and ruleth; but that which is actuated or operated, is ruled.

29. And that which ruleth, directeth, and governeth as free, but the other is ruled, a servant.

30. Acts or Operations, do not only actuate or operate, living or breathing, or insouled {(ἐμψυχα)} Bodies, but also Breathless Bodies, or without Souls, Wood, and Stones, and such like, increasing, and bearing fruit, ripening, corrupting, rotting, putrifying, and breaking, or working such like things, and whatsoever inanimate Bodies can suffer.

31. Act or Operation, O Son, is called, whatsoever is, or is made or done, and there are always many things made, or rather all things.

32. For the World is never widowed or forsaken of any of those things that are, but being always carried or moved in itself, it is in labour to bring forth the things that are, which shall never be left by it to corruption.

33. Let, therefore, every Act or Operation be understood to be always Immortal, in what manner of Body soever it be.

34. But some Acts or Operations be of Divine, some of corruptible Bodies, some universal, some peculiar, and some of the generals, and some of the parts of everything.

35. Divine Acts or Operations, therefore, there be, and such as work or operate upon their proper Bodies, and these also are perfect, and being upon or in perfect Bodies.

36. Particular are they which work by any of the living Creatures.

37. Proper, be they that work upon any of the things that are.

38. By this Discourse, therefore, O Son, it is gathered that all things are full of Acts or Operations.

39. For if necessarily they be in every Body, and that there be many Bodies in the World, I may very well affirm, that there be many other Acts or Operations.

40. For many items in one Body, there is one, and a second, and a third, besides these universal ones that follow.

41. And universal Operations, I call them that are indeed bodily, and are done by the Senses and Motions.

42. For without these, it is impossible that the Body should consist.

43. But other Operations are proper to the Souls of Men, by Arts, Sciences, Studies, and Actions.

44. The Senses also follow these Operations, or rather are the effects or perfections {(ἀποτελέσμαγα)} of them.

45. Understand, therefore, O Son, the difference of Operations, it is sent from above.

46. But Sense being in the Body, and having its essence

from it, when it receiveth Act or Operation, manifesteth it, making it as it were Corporeal.

47. Therefore, I say, that the Senses are both Corporeal and mortal, having so much existence as the Body, for they are born with the Body, and die with it.

48. But mortal things themselves have not Sense, as Not consisting of such an Essence.

49. For Sense can be no other than a corporeal apprehension, either of Evil or Good, that comes to the Body.

50. But to External Bodies there is nothing comes, nothing departs: therefore there is no Sense in them.

51. Tat:—Doth the Sense therefore perceive or apprehend in every Body?

52. Hermes:—In every Body, O Son.

53. Tat:—And do the Acts or Operations work in all things?

54. Hermes:—Even in things inanimate, O Son, but there are differences of Senses.

55. For the Senses of things rational, are with Reason; of things unreasonable, Corporeal only, but the Senses of things inanimate, are passive only, according to Augmentation and Diminution.

56. But Passion and Sense depend both upon one head, or height, and are gathered together into the same, by Acts or Operations.

57. But in living wights, there be two other Operations that follow the Senses and Passions, to wit, Grief and Pleasure.

58. And without these, it is impossible that a living wight, especially a reasonable one, should Perceive or Apprehend.

59. And, therefore, I say, that these are the Ideas of Passions that bear rule, especially in reasonable living wights.

60. The Operations work indeed, but the Senses do declare and manifest the Operations, and they being bodily, are moved by the brutish parts of the Soul; therefore, I say, they are both maleficial, or doers of Evil.

61. For that which affords the Sense to rejoice with Pleasure, is strightway the cause of many evils, happening to him that suffers it.

62. But Sorrow gives stronger torments, and Anguish, therefore, doubtless, are they both maleficial.

63. The same may be said of the Sense of the Soul.

64. TAT:—Is not the Soul incorporeal, and the Sense a Body, Father? Or is it rather in the Body?

65. HERMES:—If we put it in a Body, O Son, we shall make it like the Soul, or the Operations, for these being unbodily, we say are in Bodies.

66. But Sense is neither Operation, nor Soul, nor anything else that belongs to the Body, but as we have said, and therefore it is not incorporeal.

67. And if it be not incorporeal, it must needs be a Body; for we always say, that of things that are, some are Bodies, and some incorporeal.

THE END OF

THE FOURTEENTH BOOK.

# THE FIFTEENTH BOOK,

CALLED

## "OF TRUTH TO HIS SON TAT."

———

HERMES:—OF TRUTH, O Tat, it is not possible that man, being an imperfect wight, compounded of Imperfect Members, and having his Tabernacle, consisting of different, and many Bodies, should speak with any Confidence.

2. But as far as it is possible, and just, I say, That Truth is only in Eternal Bodies, whose very Bodies are also True.

3. The Fire is fire itself only, and nothing else; the Earth is earth itself, and nothing else; the Air is air itself, and nothing else; the Water, water itself, and nothing else.

4. But our Bodies consist of all these; for they have of the Fire, they have of the Earth, they have of the Water, and Air, and yet there is neither Fire, nor Earth, nor Water, nor Air, nor anything True.

5. And if at the Beginning, our Constitution had not Truth, how could men either see the Truth, or speak it, or understand it only, except God would?

6. All things, therefore, upon Earth, O Tat, are not Truth, but imitations of the Truth, and yet not all things neither, for they are but few that are so.

7. But the other things are Falsehood, and Deceit, O Tat, and Opinions, like the Images of the fantasy[16] or appearance.

8. And when the fantasy[17] hath an influence from above, then it is an imitation of Truth, but without that Operation from above, it is left a lie.

9. And as an Image shews the Body described, and yet it is not the Body of that which is seen, as it seems to be, and it is seen to have eyes, but it sees nothing, and ears, but it hears nothing at all; and all other things hath the picture, but they are false, deceiving the eyes of the beholder, whilst they think they see the Truth, and yet they are indeed but lies.

10. As many, therefore, as see not Falsehood, see the Truth.

11. If, therefore, we do so understand, and see every one of those things as it is, then we see and understand true things.

12. But if we see or understand anything besides, or otherwise, than that which is, we shall neither understand, nor know the Truth.

13. TAT:—Is Truth, therefore, upon Earth, O Father?

14. HERMES:—Thou dost not miss the mark, O Son, Truth indeed is nowhere at all upon Earth, O Tat, for it cannot be generated, or made.

15. But concerning the Truth, it may be that some men, to whom God will give the Good seeing Power, may understand it.

16. So that unto the Mind, and Reason, there is nothing true indeed upon Earth.

17. But unto the True Mind, and Reason, all things are fantasies,[18] or appearances, and opinions.

18. TAT:—Must we not, therefore, call it Truth, to understand and speak the things that are?

19. HERMES:—But there is nothing true upon Earth.

20. TAT:—How then is this true, That we do not know anything True? How can that be done here?

21. HERMES:—O Son, Truth is the most perfect Virtue, and the highest Good itself, not troubled by Matter, not encompassed by a Body, naked, clear, unchangeable, venerable, unalterable Good.

22. But the things that are here, O Son, are visible, incapable of Good, corruptible, passible, dissolvable, changeable, continually altered, and made of another.

23. The things therefore that are not true to themselves, how can they be True?

24. For everything that is altered, is a lie, not abiding in what it is; but being changed it shews us always, other, and other appearances.

25. Tat:—Is not man true, O Father?

26. Hermes:—As far forth as he is a Man, he is not true, Son; for that which is True, hath of itself alone its Constitution, and remains and abides according to itself, such as it is.

27. But Man consists of many things, and doth not abide of himself, but is turned and changed, age after age, Idea after Idea, or form after form, and this while he is yet in the Tabernacle.

28. And many have not known their own children after a little while, and many children likewise have not known their own Parents.

29. Is it then possible, O Tat, that he who is so changed, as is not to be known, should be True? No, on the contrary, he is Falsehood, being in many Appearance of changes.

30. But do thou understand the True to be that which abides the same, and is Eternal, but man is not ever, therefore not True, but man is a certain Appearance, and Appearance is the highest Lie or Falsehood.

31. Tat:—But these Eternal Bodies, Father, are they not True, though they be changed?

32. Hermes:—Everything that is begotten, or made, and changed, is not True; but being made by our Progenitor, they might have had true Matter.

33. But these also have in themselves, something that is False, in regard to their change.

34. For nothing that remains not in itself, is True.

35. Tat:—What shall one say then, Father, that only the Sun, which besides the Nature of other things, is not changed, but abides in itself, is Truth?

36. Hᴇʀᴍᴇꜱ:—It is Truth, and therefore is he only intrusted with the Workmanship of the World, ruling and making all things, whom I do both honour, and adore his Truth; and after the One, and First, I acknowledge him the Workman.

37. Tᴀᴛ:—What, therefore, doth thou affirm to be the first Truth, O Father?

38. Hᴇʀᴍᴇꜱ:—The One and Only, O Tat, that is not of Matter, that is not in a Body, that is without Colour, without Figure, or Shape, Immutable, Unalterable, which always is; but Falsehood, O Son, is corrupted.

39. And Corruption hath laid hold upon all things on Earth, and the Providence of the True encompasseth, and will encompass them.

40. For without Corruption there can no Generation consist.

41. For Corruption followeth every Generation, that it may again be generated.

42. For those things that are generated, must of necessity be generated of those things that are corrupted, and the things generated must needs be corrupted, that the Generation of things being, may not stand still or cease.

43. Acknowledge, therefore, the first Workman, by the Generation of things.

44. Consequently the things that are generated of Corruption are false, as being sometimes one thing, sometimes another: For it is impossible, they should be made the same things again, and that which is not the same, how is it True?

45. Therefore, O Son, we must call these things fantasies[19] or appearances.

46. And if we will give a man his right name, we must call him the appearance of Manhood; and a Child, the fantasy[20] or appearance of a Child; an old man, the {fantasy or}[21] appearance of an old man; a young man, the appearance of

a young man; and a man of ripe age, the appearance of a man of ripe age.

47. For neither is a man, a man; nor a child, a child; nor a young man, young man; nor an old man, an old man.

48. But the things that pre-exist, and that are, being changed, are False.

49. These things, understand thus, O Son, as these False Operations, having their dependence from above, even of the Truth itself.

50. Which being so, I do affirm, that Falsehood is the Work of the Truth.

THE END OF

THE FIFTEENTH BOOK.

# THE SIXTEENTH BOOK,

CALLED

## "THAT NONE OF THE THINGS
## THAT ARE, CAN PERISH."

———

HERMES:—WE must now speak of the Soul, and Body, O Son; after what manner the Soul is Immortal, and what operation that is, which constitutes the Body, and dissolves it.

2. But in none of these is Death, for it is a conception of a name, which is either an empty word, or else it is wrongly called Death {(θάνατος)}, (by taking away the first letter,) instead of Immortal {(άθάνατο)}.[22]

3. For Death is destruction, but there is nothing in the whole World that is destroyed.

4. For if the World be a second God, and an Immortal living Wight, it is impossible that any part of an Immortal living Wight should die.

5. But all things that are in the World, are members of the World, especially Man, the reasonable living Wight.

6. For the first of all is God, the Eternal, the Unmade, and the Workman of all things.

7. The second is the World, made by him, after his own Image, and by him holden together, and nourished, and immortalized; and as from its own Father, ever living.

8. So that as Immortal, it is ever living, and ever immortal.

9. For that which is ever living, differs from that which is eternal.

10. For the Eternal was not begotten, or made by another; and if it were begotten or made, yet it was made by itself, not by any other, but it is always made.

11. For the Eternal, as it is Eternal, is the Universe.

12. For the Father himself, is Eternal of himself, but the World was made by the Father, ever living, and immortal.

13. And as much Matter as there was laid up by him, the Father made it all into a Body, and swelling it, made it round like a Sphere, endued it with Quality, being itself immortal, and having Eternal Materiality.

14. The Father being full of Ideas, sowed Qualities in the Spheres, and shut them up, as in a Circle, deliberating to beautify with every Quality, that which should afterwards be made.

15. Then clothing the Universal Body with Immortality, lest the Matter, if it would depart from this Composition, should be dissolved into its own disorder.

16. For when the Matter was Incorporated, O Son, it was disordered, and it hath here the same confusion daily revolved about other little things, endued with Qualities, in point of Augmentation, and Diminution, which men call Death, being indeed a disorder happening about earthly living wights.

17. For the Bodies of Heavenly things, have one order, which they have received from the Father at the Beginning, and is by the instauration of each of them, kept indissolvable.

18. But the instauration of earthly Bodies, is their consistence; and their dissolution restores them into indissoluble,[23] that is, Immortal.

19. And so there is made a privation of Sense, but not a destruction of Bodies.

20. Now the third living wight is Man, made after the Image of the World; and having by the Will of the Father, a Mind above other earthly wights.

21. And he hath not only a sympathy with the second God, but also an understanding of the first.

22. For the Second God, he apprehends as a Body; but the first, he understands as Incorporeal, and the Mind of the Good.

23. TAT:—And doth not this living wight perish?

24. HERMES:—Speak advisedly, O Son, and learn what God is, what the World, what an Immortal Wight, and what a dissolvable One is.

25. And understand that the World is of God, and in God; but Man of the World, and in the World.

26. The Beginning, and End, and Consistence of all, is God.

THE END OF

## THE SIXTEENTH BOOK.

# THE SEVENTEENTH BOOK,

## "TO ASCLEPIUS, TO BE TRULY WISE."

———

BECAUSE, my Son, Tat, in thy absence, would needs learn the Nature of the things that are: He would not suffer me to give over (as coming very young to the knowledge of every individual), till I was forced to discourse to him many things at large, that his contemplation might, from point to point, be more easy, and successful.

2. But to thee, I have thought good to write in few words, choosing out the principal heads of the things then spoken, and to interpret them more mystically, because thou hast, both more years, and more knowledge of Nature.

3. All things that appear, were made, and are made.

4. Those things that are made, are not made by themselves, but by another.

5. And there are many things made, but especially all things that appear, and which are different, and not like.

6. If the things that be made and done, be made and done by another, there must be one that must make, and do them; and he, unmade, and more ancient than the things that are made.

7. For I affirm the things that are made, to be made by another; and it is impossible, that of the things that are made, any should be more ancient than all, but only that which is not made.

8. He is stronger, and One, and only knowing all things indeed, as not having anything more ancient than himself.

9. For he bears rule, both over multitude and greatness, and the diversity of the things that are made, and the continuity of the Facture, and of the Operation.

10. Moreover, the things that are made, are visible, but he is invisible; and for this cause, he maketh them, that he may be visible; and therefore he makes them always.

11. Thus, it is fit to understand, and understanding to admire, and admiring to think thyself happy, that knowest thy natural Father.

12. For what is sweeter than a Natural Father?

13. Who, therefore, is this, or how shall we know him?

14. Or is it just to ascribe unto him alone, the Title and Appellation of God, or of the Maker, or of the Father, or of all Three? That of God because of his Power; the Maker, because of his Working and Operation; and the Father, because of his Goodness.

15. For Power is different from the things that are made, but Act or Operation, in that all things are made.

16. Wherefore, letting go all much and vain talking, we must understand these two things, That Which is made, and Him Which is the Maker; for there is nothing in the Middle, between these Two, nor is there any third.

17. Therefore, understanding All things, remember these Two; and think that these are All things, putting nothing into doubt; neither of the things above, nor of the things below; neither of things changeable, nor things that are in darkness or secret.

18. For All things, are but Two Things, That which Maketh, and that which is Made; and the One of them cannot depart, or be divided from the Other.

19. For neither is it possible that the Maker should be without the thing made, for either of them is the self-same thing; therefore cannot the One of them be separated from the other, no more than a thing can be separated from itself.

20. For if he that makes be nothing else, but that which makes alone, Simple, Uncompounded, it is of necessity, that he makes the same thing to himself, to whom it is the Generation of him that maketh to be also All that is made.

21. For that which is Generated or made, must necessarily be generated or made by another, but without the Maker, that which is made, neither is made, nor is; for the one of them without the other, hath lost his proper Nature by the privation of the other.

22. So if these Two be confessed, That which maketh, and that which is made, then they are One in Union, this going before, and that following.

23. And that which goeth before, is, God the Maker, and that which follows is, that which is made, be it what it will.

24. And let no man be afraid because of the variety of things that are made or done, lest he should case an aspersion of baseness, or infamy upon God, for it is the only Glory of him to do, or make all things.

25. And this making, or Facture, is as it were the Body of God, and to him that maketh, or doth, there is nothing evil or filthy to be imputed, or There is Nothing thought Evil, or Filthy.

26. For these are Passions that follow Generation, as Rust doth Copper, or as Excrements do the Body.

27. But neither did the Copper-smith make the Rust, nor the Maker of the Filth, nor God the Evilness.

28. But the vicissitude of Generation doth make them, as it were, to blossom out; and for this cause did make Change to be, as one should say, The Purgation of Generation.

29. Moreover, is it lawful for the same Painter to make both Heaven, and the Gods, and the Earth, and the Sea, and Men, and brute Beasts, and inanimate Things, and Trees; and is it impossible for God to make these things? O the great madness, and ignorance of men in things that concern God!

30. For men that think so, suffer that which is most ridiculous of all; for professing to bless, and praise God, yet in not ascribing to him the making or doing of All things, they know him not.

31. And besides their not knowing him, they are extremely impious against him, attributing unto him Passions, as Pride, or Oversight, or Weakness, or Ignorance, or Envy.

32. For if he do not make, or do all things, he is either proud, or not able, or ignorant, or envious, which is impious to affirm.

33. For God hath only one Passion, namely, Good; and he that is good, is neither proud, nor impotent, nor the rest, but God is Good itself.

34. For Good is all Power, to do or make all things, and everything that is made, is made by God, that is, by the Good, and that can make or do all things.

35. See, then, how he maketh all things, and how the things are done, that are done, and if thou wilt learn, thou mayest see an Image thereof, very beautiful, and like.

36. Look upon the Husbandman, how he casteth Seeds into the Earth, here Wheat, there Barley, and elsewhere some other Seeds.

37. Look upon the same Man, planting a Vine, or an Apple Tree, or a Fig Tree, or some other Tree.

38. So doth God in Heaven sow Immortality, in the Earth, Change in the whole Life and Motion.

39. And these things are not many, but few, and easily numbered, for they are all but four, God and Generation, in which are all things.

THE END OF

THE SEVENTEENTH BOOK.

# NOTES

## "DIVINE PYMANDER."

———

1. The Robert H. Fryar 1884 edition used "desired," the Westcott 1894 edition used "deified."–D.K.

2. Sentences in fancy brackets "{ }" were in the Robert H. Fryar 1884 edition and not in the Westcott 1894 edition.–D.K.

3. The Robert H. Fryar 1884 edition used "Stronger," and the Westcott 1894 edition used "Greater."–D.K.

4. Very imperfect, but is identical with all former Translations and Editions, and which, I believed, would be considered more generally acceptable if presented in its original facsimile rendering, than supplemented (as was suggested) by any additions from current Modern "Spiritual" Mediumistic sources. –R.H.F.

5. The Westcott edition used "Divine and Human," and the Robert H. Fryar edition used "Divine and Humane." I have decided to use the Fryar edition.–D.K.

6. The Westcott edition used "Son," and the Robert H. Fryar edition used "Sun." I have decided to use the Fryar edition.–D.K.

7. The Robert H. Fryar edition used "unstrained sight" and the Westcott edition used "unfeigned sight."–D.K.

8. The Robert H. Fryar edition used "high" and the Westcott edition used "bright."–D.K.

9. The Robert H. Fryar edition used "now" and the Westcott edition used "thou."–D.K.

10. The Robert H. Fryar edition used "Savour" and the Westcott edition used "favour."–D.K.

11. The Robert H. Fryar edition used "A Body perpetual" and the Westcott edition used "A Body immarcessible."–D.K.

12. The Robert H. Fryar edition used "seeing" and the Westcott edition used "feeling."–D.K.

13. The Robert H. Fryar edition used "of being" and the Westcott edition used "to be."–D.K.

14. The Robert H. Fryar edition used "eared" and the Westcott edition used "saved."–D.K.

15. The Robert H. Fryar edition used "being" and the Westcott edition used "seeing."–D.K.

16. The Robert H. Fryar edition used "fancy of appearance" and the Westcott edition used "fantasy or appearance."–D.K.

17. The Robert H. Fryar edition used "fancy" and the Westcott edition used "fantasy."–D.K.

18. The Robert H. Fryar edition used "fancies" and the Westcott edition used "fantasies."–D.K.

19. See Note 18.–D.K.

20. See Note 17.–D.K.

21. See Note 17.–D.K.

22. "Thanatos" [Death] was used for "Athanatos" [Immortal].–W.W.W.

23. The Robert H. Fryar edition used "indissolvable" and the Westcott edition used "indissoluble."–D.K.

# APPENDIX I:

## Advertisements for the
### "Divine Pymander" (1884)

# SPECIAL NOTICE.

OCCULT, THEOSOPHICAL, AND ADVANCED THINKERS are hereby informed, that an unique Illustrated Subscription Reprint Edition is in preparation of, that world-famous Initiate's Master-piece, "THE DIVINE PYMANDER," of "HERMES TRISMEGISTUS"; prefaced with an Introduction, as also a specially-written Preliminary Essay, by that distinguished Esoteric *Litterateur*, HARGRAVE JENNINGS, author of the "Rosicrucians," &c., &c.

Manetho, Herodotus, and other ancient historians speak of the writings of the Egyptian HERMES, whose very existence is lost in the night of time. Ages before Abraham pitched his tents upon the plains of Mamre, or Lot wandered on the banks of the Jordan, these Hermetic Writings formed the Sacred Books of the Egyptian Priesthood. Those who wish to know from what source Moses (who was educated according to all the wisdom of the Egyptians) obtained the material to construct the Pentateuch, should read this sacred volume. It deals with Mind, Matter, Creation and the Immortality of the Human Soul, in a masterly manner. These Hermetic Writings have been confined for ages to those secret Brotherhoods of the past, so ably spoken of by Mr. W. Oxley, and the late Henry Melville in his remarkable book "VERITAS," and are now about to be made the common property of a limited number of minds, that are sufficiently progressed to appreciate the Mystical Wisdom of Ancient Egypt, to know the past, and by the Infallible Hermetic Laws read the future, should immediately apply to prevent disappointment, as the number of Copies will be limited to the exact number of Subscribers, and the List will close in five weeks time for Great Britian, and two month for the United States.

Prospectus from ROBT. H. FRYAR, M.B.A. Bath, March 1st, 1884.

## Advertisement for "Divine Pymander" No. I
*The Medium & Daybreak of Spiritualism.* Vol. XV; No. 734, (1884).

"THE DIVINE PYMANDER."

To the Editor.—Dear Sir.—In my notice now appearing, are the reprint of the above, two alterations appear desirable, viz: "Secret Brotherhood of the Past," should be "Secret Brothers of the Orient "—and again, "a limited number of minds that are," etc., should be "a limited number of minds—those that are sufficiently progressed," etc.

Trusting intending subscribers will at once enter their names, as the edition of this Oriental chef d'œuvre of Eastern esoteric literature of 1650 will be strictly limited to 200 copies, and which are being both eagerly and rapidly secured, ——I remain, yours truly, ROBERT H. FRYAR. Bath, March 18.

## Advertisement for "Divine Pymander" No. II
*The Medium & Daybreak of Spiritualism.* Vol. XV; No. 734, (1884).

"THE DIVINE PYMANDER."

To the Editor.—Dear Sir,—Though desirous in every way of promoting and extending to all that latitude in freedom both of action and expression which is so dear to us all, I would ask the favour of space enough to say, that no other edition of the above work, but that of my own copyright, contains the much sought after and scholarly paper on "Hermes Trismegistus" (by Hargrave Jennings, author of "the Rosicrucians," "Phallicism," etc.), and without which it cannot be considered perfect. My reason for stating this is that another in every way inferior publication is I hear to be published, If not already so, and it would be unjust to my subscribers, as also to the friends of the movement, not to warn them against an edition, which they might otherwise mistake for mine, on which it is the universal testimony that there has been no effort spared, time or money, to constitute it The Hermetic Lux chef d'ouvre for this generation, and of which there is about 20 copies still left.—Yours truly,

Bath. ROBT. H. FRYAR.

## Advertisement for "Divine Pymander" No. III
*The Medium & Daybreak of Spiritualism.* Vol. XV; No. 763, (1884).

THE INITIAL VOLUME OF THE

# Bath Occult Reprint Series

(PROPRIETARY).

## ROBT. H. FRYAR, BATH.

---

# "THE DIVINE PYMANDER,"

## By Hermes Mercurius Trismegistus,

Uniquely printed in Old Face Type, on Antique Hand-made Whatman paper, post quarto, from the text of Dr. EVERARD, Ed. 1650. In Seventeen Chapters, with a choice Symbolical Cabalistic Frontispiece. Title-Page in two colours, and a fac-simile of the Smaragdine Table ; also a specially written Introduction and Preliminary Essay, by "Hargrave Jennings," author of the "Rosicrucians," "Phallicism," etc.

The work is not only valuable for its antiquity, but for the view it affords of the mind in the absence of direct revelation, searching after the "unknown God," spoken of by Paul, whom the Greeks ignorantly worshipped. This, as well as other mystical works, shows the necessity of a revelation of God in humanity. The mind in its attempt to define the Infinite and the unconditioned, has befogged itself with words of learned length, which have not even satisfied those who have used them. Learned and devout Christians contend that we cannot conceive of any higher being than a man, and of any higher man than Christ Jesus, in "whom dwelleth all the fulness of the Godhead bodily." In other words, that God clothed Himself with humanity to bring Himself down to the apprehension of mankind. By way of contrast to this simple statement of Christian belief, the Pymander, or Poemander, is very instructive and suggestive. As a literary curiosity, if nothing more, it is worthy a place in every library, and must be very interesting to those who love the mysterious.

The flattering success and encouragement accorded to the Editor by the Subscribers to the above, also the *Indian Theosophist*, and other current advanced sources, has induced the effort for their continuation, in the issue of the subjoined list of specially selected *chef-d'œuvres* of Continental Occult Literature, for Translation and Publication in English, in strictly limited editions if the demand for all, or either, sufficiently indicate the necessity of this new departure, and guarantee its advisability.

Advertisement for "Divine Pymander" No. IV
*Mental Magic.* George Redway, (1884).

# Bath Occult Reprint Series.

A list of specially selected *chef-d'œuvres* of Continental Occult Literature, for Translation and Publication in English, in strictly limited editions if the demand for all, or either, sufficiently indicate the necessity of this new departure, and guarantee its advisability.

Printed uniform in size with the present Volume.

---

**No. 2.**   HERMES'
## "VIRGIN OF THE WORLD,"
*(An Hermetic Allegory,)*
The Companion Volume to "Divine Pymander," at a special price, only to Subscribers of "Hermes" reprints, by direct application to Editor.

---

**No. 3.**   L. A. CAHAGNETS,
## MAGNETIC MAGIC.
A Repertoire of Cabbalism, Mirrors, Suspension Conveyed, Pacts, Talismans, Spells, Possessions, Sorcery, Magic, Necromancy, etc. An unique practical Work for all who aspire to proficiency in Seership, Clairvoyance, Occult Knowledges, and Powers.

---

**No. 4.**   ELIPHAS LEVI
*(The Abbe Constant),*
## "THE KEY TO THE GRAND MYSTERIES"
(The Masterpiece of French Magical Works).

---

**No. 5.**   "BARON DUPOTET,"
## "MAGIC UNVEILED"
(Sold by the Author to his *pupils only* at the prohibitive price of 100 Francs).

---

Immediate attention is therefore earnestly requested, that the probable number of copies required, their prices, etc., may be approximately ascertained and communicated to intending Subscribers.

Address, enclosing stamp for reply to Editor,

# ROBT. H. FRYAR, BATH,

From whom a few surplus copies of the "DIVINE PYMANDER" (the Initial Volume of the Bath Occult Reprint Series) can be privately obtained.

*N.B.—Personal Interviews declined.*

---

THE THEOSOPHIST. A Monthly Journal devoted to Science, Oriental Philosophy, History, Psychology, Literature, and Art. Conducted by H. P. Blavatsky. Subscription, £1 per annum, post free. Post Office Orders to "The Proprietors of 'The Theosophist,'" Adyar P.O., Madras, India.

Advertisement for "Divine Pymander" No. V
*Divine Pymander.* George Redway, (1884).

# APPENDIX II:

## Advertisement for
## "Students of the Occult Science"

### ☞ TO WHOM IT MAY CONCERN.

STUDENTS of the Occult Science, searchers after truth, and Theosophists who may have been disappointed in their expectations of Sublime Wisdom being freely dispensed by HINDOO MAHATMAS, are cordially invited to send in their names to the Editor of this Work, when, if found suitable, can be admitted, after a short probationary term, as Members of an Occult Brotherhood, who do not boast of their knowledge or attainments, but teach freely and without reserve all they find worthy to receive.

N.B.—All communications should be addressed

"THEON," c. o. ROBT. H. FRYAR,
[BATH.

Advertisement for "Students of the Occult Science"
*Divine Pymander*. George Redway, (1884).

# APPENDIX III:

## Advertisements for the "Collectanea Hermetica" Series

THEOSOPHICAL PUBLISHING SOCIETY; LONDON, AND NEW YORK.

31. *The Pymander of Hermes*, 1894, 3/, is the second volume of "Collectanea Hermetica," edited by W. WYNN WESTCOTT, is a reprint, with verbal alterations, of the translation made in the seventeenth century, by the Revd. John Everard, D.D., from an Arabic text. The work is found in various languages, but is rather scarce; and if there be a demand for such, the present edition will be found to meet it satisfactorily.

### Advertisement for "Collectanea Hermetica" No. I
*The Imperial & Asiatic Quarterly Review.* Vol. VIII; No. 15, (1894).

#### *Books, Pamphlets, and Exchanges.*

COLLECTANEA HERMETICA. Vol. IV, Æsch Mezareph or Purifying Fire. A Chymico-Kabalistic Treatise collected from the Kabala Denudata of Knorr Von Rosenroth. Translated by a Lover of Philalethes, 1714. Preface, notes and explanations by "SAPERE AUDE." Edited by W. WYNN WESTCOTT, M. B., D. P. H. S. M. of the Soc. Rosic. in Anglia. W. M. of the Quartuor Coronati Lodge. Published by Theosophical Publishing Society, 7 Duke Street, Adelphi, London, W. C., England. 1894. 12mo. pp. 60. Price, two shillings and six pence. This is the fourth volume of the "Collectanea Hermetica." The four volumes thus far published are entitled as follows :
  Vol. I. Hermetic Arcanum of Penes Nos Unda Tagi, 1623.
  Vol. II. The Divine Pymander of Hermes, preface by the editor.
  Vol. III. Short Enquiry Concerning the Hermetic Art, 1714.
  Vol. IV. Æsch Mezareph or Purifying Fire.
  Prices : Vols. I, III, and IV, two shillings and sixpence each; Vol. II, three shillings. Future volumes to be published : " The Dream of Scipio," with notes by L. O. " The Golden Verses of Pythagoras," prepared by A. E. A. Send orders to the publishers of the series ; or to " The Path," Box 2659, New York City ; or to the Occult Publishing Co., Box 2646, Boston, Mass. ; or to this office.

### Advertisement for "Collectanea Hermetica" No. II
*Miscellaneous Notes and Queries.* Vol. XIII; No. 1, (1895).

# COLLECTANEA HERMETICA

VOLUME I.

## The Hermetic Arcanum of Jean d'Espagnet

PREFACE AND NOTES BY S. A.

*Price 2s. 6d. net.*

---

VOLUME II.

## The Divine Pymander of Hermes

*Price 3s. net.*

---

VOLUME III.

*(In preparation)*

## A Short Enquiry concerning the Hermetic Art. 1714, Anon.

INTRODUCTION AND NOTES BY S. S. D. D.

*Price 2s. 6d. net.*

---

VOLUME IV.

## The Dream of Scipio

WITH NOTES BY L. O.

## The Golden Verses of Pythagoras

PREPARED BY A. E. A.

*Price not fixed.*

THEOSOPHICAL PUBLISHING SOCIETY
7, DUKE STREET, ADELPHI, LONDON, W.C.

Advertisement for "Collectanea Hermetica" No. III
*Divine Pymander.* Theosophical Publishing Society, (1894).

# APPENDIX IV:

## Review of the "Collectanea Hermetica" Series

COLLECTANEA HERMETICA.—Edited by Dr. W.
Wynn Westcott, Theosophical Publishing
Society, 7 Duke Street, Adephi, W.C. Price
2s. 6d. to 3s. 6d. per vol. net.

Under this title is now being published "a series
of annotated reprints of curious old tracts upon
Hermetic, Rosicrucian, and Alchymic subjects."
Many of these ancient treaties contain pearls of
truth which the modern students is but too apt to
ignore, tough connected with occult facts of the
highest importance. The general editor is well
knowu as an erudite Scholar; and from his official
position as Supreme Magus of the SOCIETAS
ROSICRUCIANA IN ANGLIA, is able to obtain the
assistance of those best qualified to edit each
particular volume.

The first treatise is a new and more accurate
translation from the original Latin, of the ARCANUM
HERMETICÆ PHILOSOPHIÆ OPUS, published in 1623
by Jean d'Espagnet. It is a valuable and suggestive essay on Alchymy, edited by "Sapere
Aude," a Frater of the Order of R.R. et A.C., and
enriched by notes from various Adepti.

The second volume is edited by Dr. Westcott
himself, and is a reprint of Dr. Everard's translation from the Arabic of the DIVINE PYMANDER of
Hermes, a work embodying much of the sublime
spiritual philosophy of past ages.

The third is entitled "A Short Enquiry concerning the Hermetic Art," originally published in 1714. This also treats on Alchymy, in a clearer manner than is frequently the case; and is still further elucidated by a Preface from "Non Omnis Moriar," and an Introduction and Notes by S.S.D.D., a learned Frater and Soror respectively of the Rosicrucian Order.

These, and the forthcoming volumes of the series are worthy of the deepest study by occultists, for they contain much to be found nowhere else. Of late years there have been a tendency to assume that all real occult teaching comes from the East, and the voluminous writings of the late Madame Blavatsky have tended to enforce this view. But the Western Schools possess at least equal knowledges, and, moreover, teach them in a manner more adapted to the Western mind. As "Non Omnis Moriar" says in his preface, "From the Eastern Light which had dawned upon her [H.P.B.] so generously, she could indeed criticise, but could never fully comprehend the nature of Kabbalistic illumination."

RESURGAM, Fra. R.R. et A.C.[1]

## Review of "Collectanea Hermetica"
The Unknown World. Edted by A.E. Waite. Vol. I; No. 1, (1894).

Note:
1. This review was written by Dr. Edmund Berridge using his Golden Dawn motto "Resurgam" which translates as "I shall arise again." He joined the Golden Dawn in May 1889, but his first request for membership in April 1888 was declined.—D.K.

# BIBLIOGRAPHY

*Mercurii Trismegisti Pimander, seu Liber de Potestate et Sapientia Dei,* [The Book of the Power and Wisdom of God]. Latin translation by Marsilio Ficino. Tarviso, Gerardus de Lisa, 1471.

*Pymander de potestate et sapientia Dei.* (Ficino Latin.) Ejusdem Asclepius. Basileæ, 1532.

*Mercurii Trismegisti Poemander, seu de potestate ac sapientia divina: Aesculapii Definitiones ad Ammonem regem.* (First Greek text printed with Latin translation.) Edited by P. Angelo da Barga. Apud Adr. Turnebus. Paris, 1554.

*Deux Livres de Mercure Trismegiste Hermés tres ancien Theologien, et excellant Philosophe. L'un de la puissance et Sapience de Dieu. L'autre de la volonte de Dieu. Auecq'un Diaogue de Loys Lazarel, poëts Chrestien, intitulé le Bassin d'Hermés.* First French translation of Ficino Latin by Gabriel du Preau. Paris, 1557.

*Mercurii Trismegisti Pimander sive Poemander.* (Greek and Latin.) Franciscus Flussatio Candalæ. Bordeaux, 1574.

*Le Pimandre de Mercure Trismégiste, de la philosophie chrestienne, cognoissance du Verbe divin.* Bordeaux, 1587.

*Nova de Universis Philosophia libris quinquaginta.* Introduction (Italian) and translation (Latin) by Francisco Patrici. Ferrara, 1591.
— Another edition. R. Meiettus. Venice, 1593.

*Pymander Mercurii Trismegisti* with Commentary by Fratris Hannibalis Rosseli Calabri ordinis Minorum Regularis obserantiæ, Theologie & Philosophie. Cracow. 1585-90. 6 vols.
— Another edition. Coloniæ, 1630. 6 books in 2 vols.

*The Divine Pymander of Hermes Mercurius Trismegistus, in Seventeen Books.* Translated formerly out of the Arabick into Greek, and the new into Latine, and Dutch, and now out of the Original into English; By that Learned Divine Dr. John Everard. London, Printed by Robert White, for Tho. Brewster and Greg. Moule, at the Three Bibles in the Poultrey, under Mildreds Church, 1650.

*Hermetis Trismegisti Poemander.* Ad fidem Codicum manu scriptorum recognovit Gustavus Parthey. Berolini, 1854.

*Hermès Trismegiste. Traduction completè, precede d'une Étude sur l'Origine des Livres Hermétiques.* By Louis Ménard. Paris, 1867.

*Hermes Mercurius Trismegistus: his Divine Pymander. Also, the Asistic mystery, the Smaragdine Table and the Song of Brahm.* Edited by P.B. Randolph. Boston, MA: Rosicrucian Publishing Co., 1871.
– Another edition. OH: Randolph Publishing Co., 1889.

*The Divine Pymander of Hermes Mercurius Trismegistus.* Translated from the Arabic by Dr. Everard. (1650) Edited with introduction and preliminary essay, by Hargrave Jennings. London: Redway for Robert H. Fryar, 1884. Bath Occult Reprints I.

*Collectanea Hermetica Vol. II: The Pymander of Hermes.* Contains the Everard 1650 text. Edited with a Preface by W. Wynn Westcott. London: Theosophical Publishing Society, 1894.

*Thrice-Greatest Hermes: Studies in Hellenistic Theosophy and Gnosis.* Translations by G.R.S. Mead. London: Theosophical Publishing Society, 1906.

*The Divine Pymander of Hermes Mercurius Trismegistus; an endeavour to systematise and elucidate the Corpus Hermeticum.* By the editors of Shrine of Wisdom. London: Shrine of Wisdom, 1923.

*Hermetica: the ancient Greek and Latin writings which contain religious or philosophic teachings ascribed to Hermes Trismegistus.* Edited by Walter Scott. Oxford: Clarendon Press, 1924-36.

# NOTES

ON THE

# "CONTRIBUTORS."

Charles "Chic" Cicero has authored books on subjects including the Golden Dawn, Tarot, and ceremonial magic with his wife, S. Tabatha Cicero. Chic is the G.H. Imperator of the Hermetic Order of the Golden Dawn, an international Order with temples in several countries. He is also a member of several Masonic, Martinist, and Rosicrucian organizations. Having established a Golden Dawn temple in 1977, Chic was one of the key people who helped Regardie resurrect a legitimate, initiatory branch of the Hermetic Order of the Golden Dawn in the United States with a series of initiations performed by Regardie in the early 1980s. He met his wife and co-author, Sandra Tabatha Cicero, shortly thereafter.

Sandra Tabatha Cicero is the G.H. Cancellaria of the Hermetic Order of the Golden Dawn. She is also the Supreme Magus (Imperatrix) of the Societas Rosicruciana in America. Tabatha met her husband and co-author Chic Cicero in the early 1980s and the Golden Dawn system of magic has been her primary spiritual focus ever since.

Robert A. Gilbert has written extensively on Western Esotericism, particularly on occultism and esoteric Freemasonry during the Victorian era. He is the author of a long series of works on the Hermetic Order of the Golden Dawn and its major personalities, including both a biography and bibliography of A.E. Waite, and the definitive edition of *The House of the Hidden Light*, a joint work of Waite and Arthur Machen. He is currently writing on aspects of mysticism and of early Gnosticism. Dr. Gilbert read Philosophy and Psychology at the University of Bristol and received his doctorate from the University of London. He is also the editor of *The Christian Parapsychologist*.

DARCY KÜNTZ is the director of the Golden Dawn Research Trust which was founded in 1998. The Research Trust is preserving the teachings, ritual, history, practices, documents, letters, and books of the Hermetic Order of the Golden Dawn (as it existed between the dates 1887-1930). We are preserving this material so that the information may be available and remain accessible to scholars now and in the future. Some of his published work includes: *Complete Golden Dawn Cipher Manuscript* (1996); *Golden Dawn Sourcebook* (1996); *The Historic Structure of the Original Golden Dawn Temples* (1999); *The Golden Dawn American Source Book* (2000); *Sent From the Second Order* (2005); *Ancient Texts of the Golden Rosicrucians* (2008).

WILLIAM WYNN WESTCOTT was one of the founders of the Order of the Golden Dawn. In the Order he used the motto V.H. Frater "Sapere Aude", which translates as "Dare to be wise". Westcott was involved in a number of Orders some of which are the Societas Rosicruciana In Anglia, Freemasonry, and the Coronati Lodge #2076, the premier Lodge of Masonic Research. Westcott wrote many medical and therapeutic works, but he is better known by his Masonic and Rosicrucian works, among them are: *The Sepher Yetzirah*; *The Isiac Tablet of Cardinal Bembo*; *An Essay on Alchemy*; *Numbers, Their Occult Power and Mystic Virtues*; *The Hieroglyphic Figures of Nicholas Flamel*, and numerous volumes of the *Collectanea Hermetica*.

www.ingramcontent.com/pod-product-compliance
Lightning Source LLC
Chambersburg PA
CBHW020400100426
42812CB00001B/132